THE **WHYS** WAY

Your
TO SUCCESS
AND HAPPINESS

Betsy Speicher

Betsy Speicher

Published 2015
Printed in the USA

ISBN-13: 978-1517501105
ISBN-10: 1517501105

For information:

Sherwood Oaks Press
95 Sherwood Drive
Westlake Village, CA 91361

Dedicated to my father, Stephen, and Matt

Table of Contents

Why read this book?   1

Chapter 1   Why WHYS?   3

Chapter 2   Do you understand cause and effect?   11

Chapter 3   What are causes?   15

Chapter 4   How do you find a cause?   21

Chapter 5   Are you sure you know the cause?   33

Chapter 6   Data Mining   45

Chapter 7   WHYS emotions   57

Chapter 8   Achieving goals   75

Chapter 9   Solving problems   85

Chapter 10 The WHYS of creativity   95

Chapter 11 Teachers, experts, and advisors   105

Chapter 12 The WHYS teacher   113

Chapter 13 The WHYS Way to persuade   121

Chapter 14 Raising a WHYS child   133

Chapter 15 The WHYS and happy life   139

            Acknowledgements   147

            End Notes

WHY READ THIS BOOK?

This is the ultimate "How-To" book.

There are plenty of books on how to lose weight, make money, find your soul-mate, etc. This book will reveal the key to doing all of these by showing you how to achieve **any** goal or solve **any** problem – and much more.

Have you spent fruitless hours, days, or years trying to find the answer to an important question only to find yourself at one dead end after another with nothing to show for your efforts? Did you get distracted or sidetracked? *The WHYS Way* will show you how to focus your thinking, stay on track, and come up with the right answers.

Wouldn't it be great to really *know* what you're doing and be confident you're doing the right thing? If so, you can use *The WHYS Way*'s "Certainty Test" to determine when you can be sure and when you need more information.

Would you like to cut huge, daunting tasks down to size? *The WHYS Way* explains and demonstrates how to make effective, doable plans for your most difficult long-range projects and carry them out successfully.

Don't you wish you could avoid unpleasant outcomes when going after what you want? There are ways to anticipate and prevent unintended consequences and, if problems do occur, to solve them, cope with them, and prevent them in the future – if you know WHY the problems happened.

Why are creative geniuses inspired, struck by sudden flashes of insight, and have the answer to difficult and important questions suddenly "just come" to them? It isn't talent or luck. You can *make* it happen to *you* and have brilliant and useful ideas coming in torrents by unleashing your Creative Flow.

Can you "Google" your own vast store of information – the knowledge and experiences you've accumulated over a lifetime – and have what you want available, at your command, in an instant? You can if you use *The WHYS Way*'s "Data Miner."

This book will help you understand your emotions and WHY they are the key to achieving and preserving everything that matters the most to you. It will show you how to introspect and use your first impressions, hunches, and gut feelings effectively without being a slave to your emotions or letting them lead you astray.

In addition, *The WHYS Way* will help you in your dealings with people. While you can learn so much by listening and reading and you often need to depend on experts, others can also mislead you or take advantage of you. Who can you trust? How can you distinguish reliable teachers and advisors from fools and con-men? How can you separate great and useful ideas from nonsense? When can you rely on what others say and when should you question or reject their ideas and advice? This book will give you guidance.

The WHYS Way includes communication techniques for convincing people to buy your product or your ideas or for getting the attention and agreement of your family, friends, and co-workers. You'll also learn when someone is open to reason and when you shouldn't bother with them.

Are you now thinking: "Oh, yeah? How can one book do all that? This I gotta see."

Great! If you're skeptical of extravagant claims and bald-faced assertions, if you're an active-minded, questioning person who demands proof and expects things to make sense, *The WHYS Way* was written especially for you.

It will deliver on its promises by illustrating, step-by-step, the basic method for figuring out WHY things happen and WHY things are the way they are, based on the wisdom, reasoning methods, and example of sucessful scientists, inventors, artists, writers, philosophers, and businessmen. It will show you how to find causes and overcome errors and how to open yourself up to flashes of insight and to sudden discoveries.

Although this book deals with some heavy-duty philosophical issues, the focus is on giving you a simple set of easily-learned, practical skills with a minimum of abstract theorizing. *The WHYS Way* presents one idea at a time, proceeding systematically. You'll get plenty of familiar examples and opportunities to apply these ideas to your own goals and concerns.

Interested? Then, keep reading.

CHAPTER 1

Why WHYS?

People are always asking "Why?"

Jerry was late for work. He got in his car, turned the key, and nothing happened. "Dammit," he muttered, banging his fist against the steering wheel, "Why won't this friggin' car start?"

Mrs. Clark was delighted that Mark was doing so well in Algebra 2, since he almost flunked Algebra 1. "Why?" she asked her student. "Has something changed?"

"Why can't I have another cookie?" asked five-year-old Jake, giving his mother a plaintive look.

"Why did you talk me into that Greek bond fund?" said Sam to his broker. "I should have bought Apple stock."

In 1956, Frankie Lymon and the Teenagers sang "Why Do Fools Fall in Love?"

We are always asking "Why?" Why do we do that? What difference does knowing why make? It makes a huge difference and the whole point of this book is that:

KNOWING "WHY" IS THE KEY
TO SUCCESS AND HAPPINESS

Observe that people ask "Why?" when they need to **know** some specific, particular information for some specific, particular **purpose**. The facts and knowledge they seek will help them reach a goal, accomplish or create something, or solve a problem. This is their **cognitive purpose** – a person's motivation for knowing something.

Little Jake was after a cookie and his cognitive purpose was to learn how he could get his mother to give it to him. Once he found that out, he might be able to change her mind and get it. Sam's cognitive purposes were to make money in the stock market, determine why his broker gave him bad advice, and understand why some investments made money and others didn't.

Often someone's cognitive purpose is to solve or discover how to cope with a problem that arises in pursuit of their goals. Jerry had the long-range goal of impressing his boss and getting a raise. His cognitive purpose that morning was to find out what was wrong with his car and how to fix it quickly so he wouldn't have to look like a fool showing up late for the staff meeting.

Sometimes your cognitive purpose is simply to satisfy curiosity. A similarity between two different things piques your interest and you may look for a possible connection because finding it can have positive results. The apple pie Laura brought to the potluck dinner reminded Gene of his grandmother's pies and he wondered what gave it that delightful taste. He got Laura's recipe and now he can enjoy the pie – and the wonderful memories associated with it – any time he wants to.

Maybe something unexpected happens and you want to know why – like Mark's improvement in math. Mrs. Clark was impressed with Mark's success and hoped to find the reason for it so she could use it to help her other students.

ULTIMATE WHY = 's purpose

"WHYS" are causes and reasons

A "**WHY**" is a cause or a reason. A "WHY" might be the **cause** of an effect, of an action, or of a change, or it could be the **reason** that something is what it is. The WHY for Jerry's car not starting was that he left his headlights on overnight and his battery ran down. Mark read science fiction over the summer, which inspired him to become an engineer, and that was the WHY behind his newfound interest in algebra. Sam's broker got a bigger commission selling the bond fund than Apple stock and that was the WHY for his recommendation.

Why you need "WHYS"

You need to know WHY – causes and reasons – because …

You need to know WHY when you seek a goal.

If you want to become a physician you need to know **why** people get sick, **why** they get well, **why** some people are successful and respected practitioners of medicine, etc., and that would lead you to acquiring the knowledge you need to become a doctor. If you want to bake a cake, you'd want to know **why** a certain recipe or cake mix is the one you want.

You need to know WHY when you plan.

If you're planning a new kitchen you need to know **why** laying out the appliances a certain way will be more efficient for the way you cook, **why** pricey designer cabinets will increase the resale value of your home and justify their cost and standard ones won't, and **why** laminate floors might make more sense than wood.

If you're planning a family vacation you need to know **why** California is perfect this time of the year but Florida should be avoided (It's hurricane season), **why** a cruise is a bad idea (Your wife gets seasick), and **why** bringing along a bunch of Disney DVDs on long car trips will keep the kids from getting restless and fighting with each other in the back seat.

Whatever your goal may be, some things and actions will cause you to reach it and some will not and it's good to know **why**. When you know **why** things happen, you're better-prepared to **make** them happen. You know what you need and what you must plan for, acquire, and do to reach your goals.

You need to know WHY when you have a problem.

To successfully deal with a problem and avoid similar problems in the future, you need to determine **why** the problem happened.

Once Jerry realized that a dead battery was the reason **why** his car wouldn't start, he took out the jumper cables, got a boost from his wife's car, and was soon on his way. He also vowed to listen for the "ding, ding, ding" warning that his lights were still on when he left his car.

Stacy was one of the first people in line to buy tickets when her favorite rock group came to town, but they were already sold out. **Why** did that happen? Online purchasers and ticket scalpers had bought every last ticket long before the box office opened. Stacy realized the only way she could go to the concert was to pay a scalper twice the price, so she did, but she decided that the next time she'd buy her tickets online.

Understanding **why** you have a problem leads to real solutions rather than random, "just do something," futile activities. It reveals possible threats to what you value, promotes learning from your mistakes, and helps you to avoid repeating them.

You need to know WHY when you deal with people.

You constantly interact with others: family members and friends, co-workers, employees, and bosses, customers and clients, experts like doctors and lawyers, skilled service providers and hired help, as well as total strangers. The results can be enjoyable and profitable – or difficult and even tragic. What makes the difference is understanding the WHYS of motivation: the causes of human behavior and the reasons **why** people do what they do.

To begin with, you need to be aware of your own motivations – **why** you want what you want – and to determine, as best you can, the motivations of the people you interact with. If you're clear as to what you desire from them and can determine what they want from you, you'll know who you can and cannot trust and what you might reasonably expect to happen. You can then decide whether you should avoid some people completely or why and how you may wish to relate to them.

For example, if wealthy widow Sandra understood the depth of her own loneliness and **why** the charming young Frenchman was paying so much attention to her, she would enjoy going dancing with him but be wary of lending him money. If Mike knew **why** his sales prospect desperately wanted his product, he would begin negotiations at a much higher price.

You need to know WHY when learning from others.

Most of what you know you learned from other people: parents, teachers, writers, etc., but even the most reliable and knowledgeable people can sometimes be wrong and make mistakes. You can't be completely certain of anything you learn from others until and unless you understand **why** they say what they do. You haven't really mastered the material until you've derived or verified it yourself and understand **why** it's true.

Merely memorizing facts and concepts but not knowing **why** they are true, severely limits your ability to apply and effectively use your knowledge. As the authors of *How Learning Works: Seven Research-Based Principles for Smart Teaching* report:

It is common, for instance, for students to know facts and concepts but not know how or when to apply them. In fact, research on science learning demonstrates that even when students can state scientific facts (for example, "Force equals mass times acceleration"), they are often weak in applying those facts to solve problems, interpret data, and draw conclusions.[1]

You need to know WHY when you rely on experts.

As a bare minimum, you need to know **why** the doctor, lawyer, financial planner, or garage mechanic you consult is an expert. Sam's broker knew little about finance or investing and the certificate on his wall only proved he had completed a two-week course in how to push the securities that made the biggest profits for his employer.

You also need to know **why** the expert recommends what he does. If Sam had asked why he should buy the Greek bond fund, his broker might have said, "It's paying 20%" and, if Sam had inquired as to **why** it paid so much, he would have learned it was because the bonds were so risky – too risky for his son's college fund.

The patient who understands **why** his doctor prescribes a new drug is much better off than one who takes the medicine without knowing. He is informed about how the medicine is supposed to work and can tell his doctor if it doesn't. He is also on the alert for possible side effects and how to deal with them.

You need to know WHY when teaching your children or your students.

Nobody can learn anything unless he has a cognitive purpose. Every child or student needs a reason **why** he should care about the knowledge you want to give him. Since his cognitive purpose motivates him to learn, a parent or teacher must make sure he has one.

Mark became a top algebra student because he appreciated **why** he needed to know math to be an engineer and launch rockets. Once his teacher saw the difference having a personal cognitive purpose made, she began each new semester with a discussion of **why** space travel, video game designing, and other exciting careers require algebra.

You need to know WHY when selling a product or an idea.

Successful persuasion means showing someone **why** he should think or act as you want him to. If he already agrees with you, you merely have to point **why** what you have is what he wants or believes. If he doesn't agree, you need to find out **why** he disagrees with you before you can overcome his objections and convince him otherwise.

Charles won a Senate seat in a district his party hadn't carried for sixty years with persuasive speeches and by crushing the other candidate in debates. He won votes by explaining **why** his opponent's positions didn't make sense and would lead to consequences nobody, regardless of party or affiliation, wanted.

Rose is a master real estate saleswoman. She can size up a potential customer and determine what the buyer is looking for and **why** he wants it. She then knows exactly which properties to show, how to handle the buyer's concerns, and which features she should point out to clinch the deal.

You need to know WHY when you act.

People often fail to do the right thing or what's in their own best interests because they're unsure of themselves. They don't pursue their dreams because they're afraid they will fail. When they or their friends are attacked, they remain silent, then feel guilty that they didn't speak up. What are they lacking?

American folk hero Davy Crockett provided the answer. His motto was "Be sure you're right, and then go ahead." It's not enough to think you're right, feel you're right, or hope you're right; you have to be **sure** you're right before you can act with confidence. The way to be sure is to have a deep and solid understanding of **why** you're right.

Know-it-all Uncle Leroy usually managed to spoil family gatherings with his belligerent personal attacks on the other guests. His relatives tried to ignore him or avoid him, but no one had the courage to confront him until Cousin Dianne put him in his place. When Uncle Leroy called her favorite movie "trash that only a lowbrow would like," she didn't get defensive nor did she let it go. She told him simply, but firmly, "I don't want to hear about it. I am here to celebrate Josh's birthday, not to argue with you. This is a social occasion, not a debate forum." The cousins overheard it, smiled, and a few applauded. Uncle Leroy shut up.

Nick was a quiet and shy research scientist, but he spoke with boldness and certainty about his controversial theory in front of hundreds of biologists and physicians at the medical conference. He was prepared with all the reasons **why** his theory was true, but he wasn't always so self-assured. When he began his experiments, he wouldn't have dared to breathe a word about his hypothesis to anybody. Once the evidence was in, however, he was eager to tell the world.

You need to know WHY in order to make new discoveries.

Great scientists, inventors, and thinkers are known for discovering the WHYS that others have missed. Isaac Newton found out **why** the planets moved as they do, **why** objects fall to earth, and **why** planetary motion and falling bodies are related. Louis Pasteur discovered **why** germs cause disease and **why** heating milk, a process we now call "pasteurizing," will kill the germs.

Newton and Pasteur didn't have special access to obscure secrets of nature. They observed the same falling objects and the same sick people everyone saw. Their achievement was that they asked "Why?" and were able to find the answers.

YOUR KEY TO SUCCESS AND HAPPINESS
IS KNOWING WHY

The message of this book is that anyone can lead a more fulfilling life by focusing on the WHYS – the causes and reasons – for everything they have and want. Since that's such a desirable goal, why don't people do it already? Is it hard to do?

Actually, asking "Why?" is easy. As soon as we can talk in full sentences we begin to challenge our parents with a constant stream of questions:

"Why can't I go with you and Daddy?"

"Why do I have to eat carrots?"

But, eventually, some children give up. Their questions haven't been welcomed or they've been given answers they don't trust. They may have tried to find out why on their own, but without success.

Yet other children keep on asking and, if they don't get satisfactory explanations, they seek them out by themselves. When the process gets difficult, they persist until they find their answers and they're better than most at discovering causes and reasons for things. What makes them different?

Is it inborn talent? As Geoffrey Colvin argues in his book, *Talent Is Overrated*, what distinguishes great artists, athletes, and other outstanding performers from ordinary people is the time they spend developing their abilities and skills. They keep practicing hour after hour motivated by a desire to accomplish their goals. They succeed because they have what anyone can have: a strong cognitive purpose.

Does it take being well-educated? I'm sure you know people with heads full of facts and with graduate degrees from prestigious universities who cannot cope with the real world. They lack social skills or they can't hold down a job or manage their money. They may know many "whats" but all their learning won't help them if they lack an understanding of the WHYS.

The secret of having a solid, practical grasp of WHY isn't having a high IQ or advanced knowledge but of using the **right method**. *The WHYS Way* is that method: a method for finding and validating the causes and reasons for what happens and for what you would like to happen.

The WHYS Way is so simple that a six-year-old can learn it, but applying it well is an art. This book teaches the basic skills you can grasp and use immediately, but can improve and perfect over a lifetime.

Let's begin by looking at "cause and effect"–what you may think it means and what it **really** means.

CHAPTER 2

Do you understand cause and effect?

You probably think that you know what cause and effect is. Most people do, but their understanding is usually vague, approximate, and imprecise. That's too bad because, as we have seen, causality is involved in just about everything you do and everything that matters to you.

If you had to define cause and effect in one sentence, what would you say? Here are some typical definitions and descriptions. Which of these answers make the most sense to you?

> "Like here is an example... Cause–you trip and fall. Effect–you skin your knee."

> "It's when you do something and it makes another thing happen."

> "Cause: why something happens. Effect: what happens."

> "It's when one thing happens after another thing happens."

> "It's obvious. You just see it. When this thing happens, that thing always happens."

> "It means that when you have A, then you have to have B."

> "Cause and effect involves a relationship between one or more actions or events."

> "A cause is an action and an effect is the reaction."

Common themes

As you can see, in these everyday ideas about causality there are some similar themes:

> Causes happen before effects.

> Cause and effect is a relationship between the cause and the effect.

> Causes and their effects always go together. When two things always go together, one is the cause and one is the effect.

> Causes are actions that lead to reactions.

There's a lot of truth here, but none of these statements gets to the heart of what cause and effect actually is and all of them contain some false assumptions. As a result, you can come to mistaken conclusions and take actions that fail.

Getting causes wrong

Before and after is *not* cause and effect.

One typical error is the *post hoc* fallacy of assuming that if one thing happens after another that the first caused the second. Here's an example from *Attacking Faulty Reasoning* by T. Edward Damer:

> "I can't help but think that you are the cause of this problem; we never had any problem with the furnace until you moved into the apartment."[2]

Why would the manager of the apartment, without any evidence that the new tenant did anything at all to the furnace, assume that it was his fault that the furnace broke down? Just because he moved in right before it stopped working?

Correlation is not causation.

Many people believe that causality is nothing more than the constant correlation of two events. This view was promoted by the influential modern philosopher David Hume. He wrote that when we see two events always happening together, we confidently predict that when we see one, we will always see the other. We call one the cause and the other the effect, and we assume that there is some connection between them. We think that there is some power in the cause that never fails to produce the effect, and that this is certain and always has to happen. Thus, we assume there is a "necessary connection" between events for no other reason than that we always see them happening together.[3]

While this is often true, sometimes it isn't. Here are some false conclusions based on constant correlations, and the silly actions that might follow from them.

> The more firemen there are fighting a fire, the bigger the fire is observed to be.
>
> *Conclusion:* Firemen cause an increase in the size of a fire.
>
> *Action:* If there is a big fire, send as many firemen as possible back to the fire station.

As ice cream sales increase, the rate of drowning deaths increases sharply.

Conclusion: Ice cream consumption causes drowning.

Action: Have lifeguards at the ice cream store.

With a decrease in the wearing of hats over the past hundred years, there has been an increase in gasoline consumption over the same period.

Conclusion: Gasoline consumption is caused by people who stopped wearing hats.

Action: If you want to cut down on the use of fossil fuels, wear a hat.

Yes, all the conclusions are false, but they're all based on correlations which are true. There do tend to be more firemen at bigger fires, the number of drownings does go up in the summer and down in the winter and so do ice cream sales, and hat-wearing has diminished while gasoline consumption has increased in the past hundred years. So why are the conclusions wrong?

They're wrong because, even if A always goes with B, it doesn't mean that A **causes** B.

Sometimes B causes A. Having more firemen doesn't cause bigger fires, but a bigger fire can cause the dispatcher to call out more firemen.

Perhaps A and B aren't causally related to each other but are both caused by C. Hot weather causes people to want a nice cold ice cream treat and it also causes them to jump into a lake, a pool, or the ocean to cool off, where some of them may drown.

Maybe A and B aren't related at all and, if they occur together, it's a coincidence – like hat-wearing and gasoline consumption.

You'll find out how to avoid mistaking correlation for causation when we return to these examples in Chapter 5.

Cause and effect is not action and reaction.

The most common misconception about cause and effect – the one you probably hold – is that it's a relationship between *two actions or events* and it begins when an action (the cause) results in a reaction (the effect). One moving billiard ball strikes another stationary billiard ball (an action) and the second ball moves (the reaction). But if you think that cause and effect is just an action followed by a reaction, **where** is the cause?

According to influential philosopher David Hume, it's **nowhere**. That's because, if an action *causes* a reaction, it's not enough that the reaction merely *follows* the action. There must be a "necessary connection" between the two that *makes* the reaction happen. But what do we see?

We only see the first billiard ball move and strike the second ball, and then we see the second ball begin to move, but that's all we see. We never see any "necessary connection" between the two events. Thus, according to Hume, there's no way to tell if the action and the reaction are related at all. Maybe the whole idea of "causes" is something we just made up after seeing the two events always happening together. Maybe they don't really always *have to* happen that way.

If Hume was right and there are no causes or we can never know what they are, we're in trouble. We don't know what we can we expect of the world. And what happens to science? How can you plan and act? If you feel you're living in a world where you can never be sure of what will happen next, that's scary. Needless to say, it will undermine your self-confidence and make you afraid to do *anything*.

Getting causes right

Fortunately, when you reject Hume and understand what causes really are, these problems go away.

In the next chapter you'll find *The WHYS Way* – a different way of looking at causes that, once you get the hang of it, may seem easy and obvious. You'll see why Hume was wrong to say that you can never see "necessary connections" because a cause *isn't* a connection at all. It's something that you can perceive directly with your five senses and be sure of with some simple reasoning.

Let's see how.

CHAPTER 3

What are causes?

Causes are everywhere

Whenever you ask "Why?" you're looking for a **cause**. If you want to know why your friend is late, it means you're looking for whatever **caused** him to not show up on time. Maybe he was stuck in traffic, lost track of time, forgot the event, etc.

Whenever you use the word "because," whatever follows that word is a **causal** explanation as to why something happened. If someone says "I bought my Corvette at Heartland Chevrolet because they gave me the best price," it means that the price was what **caused** him to purchase the car at that dealership.

If you ask "How?" you're also seeking a cause. "How?" means "What will **cause** this to happen?" and the answer to a "How?" question is always a cause.

For example, there's the old joke about a young man who asks an elderly man for directions: "How do I get to Carnegie Hall?" The old man replies "Practice! Practice!" The answer the young man was expecting and the one he got were both causal. He wanted routing directions that would cause him to arrive at Carnegie Hall and the old man gave him advice that would cause him to be good enough to perform there.

If you think about it, causes are implicit in **every** statement you make and every sentence you utter. A sentence is about something – that's the subject of the sentence – and what that something is or does – which is the predicate of the sentence. Contained in the sentence is the idea that there's something about the subject that **causes** the predicate.

The statement "Jerry's car wouldn't start" means that there was something about Jerry's car (the subject) that **caused** it not to start (the predicate) – such as, perhaps, a dead battery. The generalization "All men are mortal" contains the idea that there is something about all men (the subject) that **causes** them to be mortal (the predicate).

Thus, if you want to understand the relationship between something (the subject) and what it is or does (the predicate), you need to understand cause and effect. If you want to prove or, sometimes, just make sense out of a statement, you need to be aware of causes.

What causes really are

We've seen that causes may not be just one thing happening before another or things that always go together or actions and reactions, so what are they?

Set your old assumptions aside for a while and let's look at causality in a new way. Instead of connections and reactions, *The WHYS Way* focuses on three things:

(1) **What you want** to know and do

(2) The **things** you want to understand and use

(3) The **characteristics** of things.

Those are your keys to understanding causes.

An elementary example

Imagine that we have a red ball made out of wood that's about three inches in diameter. Why does it roll when you push it? Why does it fit inside a square box that's four inches on each side? Why does it float on water? Why does it remind you of an apple?

Observe all the effects involving the little red ball: rolling, fitting, floating, etc. Each result is caused by the same object, but they're all different effects. Why is that? Let's answer the "Whys?" above and see.

The ball rolls because it's round. If it were shaped like a cube, it wouldn't. It fits inside the box because it's three inches in diameter. If the ball were five inches, all other things being equal, it wouldn't fit inside a four-inch box. It floats because it's made of wood. A similar cast iron ball would sink. It reminds you of an apple because it has the same visual characteristics – the same color, general shape, and size – as an apple.

Those are the specific characteristics of that ball – something different in each case – that account for and cause each particular effect. The ball rolls because it's round, but not because it's red. The size is important for fitting in the bigger box or making you think of an apple, but not for explaining why it floats.

For each specific effect, there is something about the ball that causes that effect.

What is true of the ball applies to **all** cause and effect relationships. There is always:

(1) **A thing.** There is always **something** that acts or changes. In our example, the thing that acts or changes is the ball. It acts by rolling or floating or changing its position from outside to inside the box or by changing your thoughts from not thinking of an apple to thinking of an apple.

(2) **Its causal characteristics.** There is always some **something about** that thing that makes it or allows it to act or change. In our ball example, depending on the particular effect we want to explain, it might be the shape of the ball, what it's made of, its size, its color, etc. A causal characteristic might be **anything** about a thing – any property or characteristic of that thing – which it **must** have in order to produce a specific effect.

(To keep it simple, from here on we will use the word "Purpose," with a capital "P," whenever we mean a purpose for knowing or what it is that you want to know or do. Likewise, we will use "Thing" to refer to the thing that acts or changes, and "Characteristic" for a causal characteristic.)

In principle:

THE CAUSE OF ANY GIVEN EFFECT ARE
THE CHARACTERISTICS OF THINGS.

That's the basic idea behind causes and, as we shall see, it's *The WHYS Way's* answer to every "Why?" or "How?" question. Why does the ball roll? Because it's a **round** (Characteristic) **object** (Thing). How does it float? **It** (the Thing) is made of **wood** (Characteristic).

If you want to know what the cause of something is, focus on the Characteristics of the Things that act or change. Ask, "What Characteristics of this Thing are the cause of this effect?"

Here are some causes explained in terms of Things and Characteristics:

Thing – The TV

Characteristics – It needs an external source of power and it's not plugged in.

Effect – When you turn the TV on, you don't get any sound or picture.

Thing – A tornado

Characteristics – It had extremely strong winds and it touched down on Third Street.

Effect – Homes were destroyed on Third Street.

Thing – A traveler.

Characteristics – She went on a Caribbean cruise and paid for it with her credit card.

Effect – She maxed out her credit card.

That's all there is to it. Just look at what things are and what they do. Understanding causes is simply a matter of identifying which things are acting, changing, or being explained – the Things – and which of their attributes and properties – their Characteristics – account for their actions, changes, or condition.

Complications

While the Thing-Characteristic view of causes is a very simple idea, some might say it's too simple. Let's look at their objections and how to answer them.

Multiple Characteristics

We just identified that the ball rolls because it's round and that definitely is a Characteristic, because the ball has to be round in order to roll. But just being round isn't enough because there are other Characteristics involved. The ball also rolls because it's made of wood. If it were made out of a non-solid material like jelly or if it were a ball of absorbent cotton, it wouldn't roll. If you want to get really picky about it, you can find additional Characteristics like the fact that the ball's temperature is below the point at which wood burns.

But generally, when answering the question, "Why does the ball roll?" we are satisfied with the answer: "Because it's round." Although we might consider additional Characteristics, we usually don't. We just focus on some Characteristics and ignore others. There's a reason for that, which we'll discuss shortly.

Multiple Things

What makes understanding causes really difficult is that there are almost always several Things interacting with each other.

If you push the ball it will roll but, if there is no outside force acting on the ball to overcome its inertia, it will just sit there. If so, rolling will require an additional Thing – in this case maybe you – with the Characteristic of being able to generate the needed force to push the ball enough to get it rolling.

The ball and something to push it are not the only Things required for it to roll. One reason our little red ball rolls on the floor is that the floor is also a Thing. The ball's rolling is an interaction with the floor, and the properties of the floor matter too. The floor has a hard, flat, level surface, but what would happen if the floor had holes in it or if it were covered in six inches of soft sand? Would the ball roll? Probably not.

But in most cases, if you want to explain why the ball rolls, pointing to the ball and what pushes it is enough even though other Things, like the floor, may be involved. By so doing, you only identify some Things and not others, and there is a good reason why you do that.

Causes of causes

Once you know the Things and what their Characteristics are, are you done? Maybe or maybe not. Causes have causes, too. Why is the ball round? Why did you push it? Why do you have the ability to push things? Everything in the universe has a cause including Things and Characteristics. You could keep on going forever – but you don't. Why?

When do you stop?

You can stop asking "Why?" when you get an answer that satisfies your Purpose.

A satisfactory answer to "Why does the ball roll?" depends on why you want to know it. For example, let's look at Joey, a toddler who wanted to find an object he could easily propel across the floor.

He tried pushing his teddy bear and some blocks and some balls. He decided that the balls work best because, when he pushed them, they went farther and faster. Joey also tried rolling a soup can and discovered that it rolled on the sides but not on the flat top and bottom. That's when he realized that the roundness is necessary for rolling. At that point he stopped asking "Why?" because he had what he wanted: roundness, the Characteristic that caused an object (Thing) to be easy to push across the floor.

Although being solid is also a Characteristic of the balls that rolled, Joey disregarded that characteristic because his blocks were also solid and, when pushed, they didn't go as fast and as far as the ball. Because he wanted to know what makes objects move easily when pushed and being solid didn't distinguish the objects that did from those that didn't, he ignored the characteristic of being solid because it was irrelevant to his Purpose.

Once you find a cause, you always have the option of continuing to look for the cause of that cause and that cause's cause etc., forever – but you don't. For one thing, life is too short. We have to stop somewhere. When can you stop looking for causes?

Just as a person's Purpose sets a limit for finding Characteristics, it also determines when he stops looking for the causes of causes. When Jerry from our previous example found out why his car didn't start, he got it jump-started and was on his way, but he also wanted to know what caused the dead battery. Since he was able to jump start it, the battery still had some life and he didn't need a new one, but as soon as the car started, he realized he had left his headlights on overnight. Because that explained why his car didn't start, his Purpose was satisfied.

Thus, whenever you ask "Why?" or "How?" you're seeking a cause and you can stop looking when you identify the causes that satisfy the Purpose of your question. To find a cause, you just have to find the right Things and Characteristics.

Looking at cause and effect *The WHYS Way* avoids many of the problems with the before-after, correlation, and action-reaction views of causality. There's no mysterious, unperceivable "necessary connection" to find, and no confusion about what caused what. You just look at what happens and ask "What Characteristics of what Things made it happen?" Then you use your five senses to look at and investigate Things and their Characteristics until you find the ones that satisfy your Purpose.

Now how do you do that?

CHAPTER 4

How do you find a cause?

What do you do when you don't know what caused something or when you can't predict what effects will happen? You figure it out using *The WHYS Way's* three main concepts: Purpose, Thing, and Characteristic.

A causal quest

When Detective Logan arrived at the crime scene, he found a body lying in a pool of blood. He saw the corpse: Nelson Winterbourne, a middle-aged businessman, shot in the back five times. Logan needed to find out whodunit – the person who **caused** the death.

Logan observed the dead body, its condition, and its location. He noted the room and its contents and the open window leading to the fire escape. He looked for, but didn't find, any sign of the murder weapon in the room.

From the position of the body and the blood stains, Logan concluded that the body hadn't been moved. The victim was in the room when he was shot and then fell close to where they found his body. The bullet wounds indicated that he was shot at close range. That meant that the killer had been in the room too, but how did he get there? The apartment door was locked and there were no signs of forced entry. Did Winterbourne know the killer and let him in?

Logan asked the doorman if anyone had called on the victim. That's when he learned that the building had security cameras focused on the hallway outside the apartment and tapes for the last 48 hours. They showed Winterbourne coming and going, but no one else.

Then Logan turned his attention to the fire escape window. It was wide open – rather odd for such a cold day – and just right for a stealthy entrance or quick exit. Logan called his assistant over. "Dust this whole area for prints, Max. See this nail sticking out of the window frame? There seems to be something caught on it. Let's take that to the lab and see if they can find some fibers and, if we really luck out, some DNA." Under the fire escape, they found a gun and Max carefully put it in a baggie.

A woman across Fifth Street reported seeing a man in a big black coat and a red baseball cap on the fire escape around the time of the murder. About ten minutes later when she was out walking her dog, she caught a glimpse of the same man heading north toward Allen Street.

A few days later the ballistics lab reported that the gun they found was, indeed, the murder weapon, and that it was registered to Winterbourne's business partner, Sherman Wilson. Emails to Wilson found on Winterbourne's computer expressed concern about large checks from the company's checking account written to unknown companies. The checks appeared to have been signed by both partners, but Winterbourne's signature was forged. Winterbourne demanded that Wilson return the funds or he would file charges with the District Attorney.

Fibers found on the nail matched a black coat with a torn left sleeve in Wilson's office closet, where they also found a red baseball cap. Wilson was arrested and charged with murder.

Analyzing the cause-finding process

The way Logan went about finding the murderer is a good example of how to find a cause and it was essentially the same process used by Joey, the toddler in our last chapter, who was trying to figure out why he could push a ball clear across the floor with very little effort.

Using these two examples, we're going to analyze the cause-finding process in great detail – in simple, obvious detail – to highlight the steps to successfully finding causes using *The WHYS Way*. You may think you already know how to do it, and you're probably right. After all, you find causes every day.

To the degree you succeed, you're probably already using *The WHYS Way*, but doing it automatically and "intuitively," without ever thinking about or understanding the process you're using. Our goal here is to make the process **conscious** so that you can control it and do it correctly, consistently, and more easily.

For instance, we all know that balls roll because they're round. It may seem to you that you always knew it but, in fact, you didn't. Children aren't born knowing that, but they learn it very early in life. If you watch a toddler playing with blocks and balls on the floor, especially the first time that he's ever done it, you'll notice he spends a lot of time rolling and pushing things, over and over. What is he doing? We're going to watch toddler Joey and analyze the process he goes through. Then we'll see how it's similar to what Logan did to find the murderer.

Later on in this book, you'll see that we're now illustrating exactly the same process that you need to solve your problems at work, make plans, and reach your goals, so hang in there. Once you get through these theoretical discussions and understand *The WHYS Way* for finding causes, you'll be able to apply them to the important practical issues of your own life.

Purposes, Things, and Characteristics

The keys to understanding the process of cause-finding are the three concepts we've already defined and discussed: Purpose, Thing, and Characteristic. Let's see how they apply to what Logan and Joey did to find their respective causes.

The starting point in cause-finding is always having a **Purpose**–a motivation to know something specific–and Logan and Joey both wanted to know what caused something.

Detective Logan wanted to find out "whodunit." The murderer he was looking for was the (causal) **Thing**–something that acts or changes to produce the effect–poor, dead Mr. Winterbourne. Joey wanted to know why he could easily push balls across the floor, but not his blocks or his teddy bear. He was looking for the **Characteristics** that make some things move better than other things. Having their respective Purposes, Logan and Joey were well on their way.

Why is having a Purpose necessary for finding a cause? When you go on a trip, you have a destination. If you don't know where you're going, you won't get there. Having a destination points you in the right direction and determines the route you'll take. Similarly, your Purpose will set the goal of your thinking and guide the process of finding your answers.

Most importantly, having a Purpose is like putting gas in your car. It provides the fuel to get you where you're going. A Purpose–the desire to know something–is an emotion and, like all emotions, it impels you to do something and gives you energy to do it. Without the fuel of a

Purpose, Logan wouldn't care enough to investigate the crime and Joey might just forget about finding out why balls roll, and take a nap instead.

What is known

Logan and Joey had their Purposes but, at first, there were important questions that remained to be answered before they could find the causes they were seeking. That's because they didn't yet know all the necessary Things and Characteristics – but they did have *some* of them.

Assessing the crime scene, Logan could see the dead body, its condition, and location, the room and its contents, and the open window leading to the fire escape. Joey had his blocks, balls, and teddy bear. As he pushed them, he observed that the balls moved easily across the floor, but the blocks and teddy bear didn't.

What is not known

Logan didn't yet know who the murderer was and Joey saw that the balls rolled and blocks didn't but he didn't know why. Logan was looking for the murderer – the Thing – while Joey wanted to know what it is about the balls – the Characteristics – that made the balls roll when the blocks didn't. Both of our cause-seekers needed to get more information, but not just any kind of information.

Looking for clues

Logan was looking for clues, but what is a clue? If we look at Logan's clues, we'll see that each one was **causally** related to the killer he is seeking. Some clues, like fingerprints and DNA, were **Characteristics** of the murderer. Some were **effects** that the killer caused like the bullet wounds indicating a shooting at close range and his image – or lack of same – on the security tapes. The gun that shot Winterbourne was a Thing and its Characteristics, like the bullets it used or where and when it was purchased, were causally related to, and could be traced back to, the killer.

Seeking Things and Characteristics

As Logan conducted his investigation of the crime scene, he paid attention to **some** things and **some** of their characteristics but not others.

He examined Winterbourne's wounds, but not his shoes. He inquired about possible visitors on the day of the crime but not about the people who had come and gone twenty years ago. Why?

Logan's Purpose set his agenda. His attention was directed by his goal – finding out whodunit – and that ruled out anything that wasn't causally related to the crime and the person who committed it. He ignored the victim's shoes, but maybe he wouldn't have if the circumstances were different. What if the victim wore pink shoelaces and there was a serial killer on the loose who only killed people wearing pink shoelaces? Then the shoes might have been causally relevant to who the killer was.

Joey, after observing that the red ball rolled and the blue ball rolled, but the red block didn't, ignored the colors of the objects and concentrated on their other properties. The standard for what Joey focused on and what he didn't was, here again, set by his Purpose.

Placeholders

Regardless of your question, if it involves a cause, you already have the answer – or at least the **formula** for your answer. Since effects are caused by the Characteristics of Things, if you know what all the relevant Things and Characteristics are, you'll have your cause. The answer to your question will always be in the form: "This effect was (or will be) caused by these Characteristics of these Things."

While that's true in general, how does it help you answer your specific question? When you don't know one or more of the effects, Characteristics, or Things, how can you even begin to think about what you don't know yet?

In math, when you have a formula but don't know the values of all the variables, you use letters like "x" and "y" to stand for the unknown values. When you want to know a cause but have unknowns, you do the same thing. **You use "placeholders" to stand for the missing effects, Things, and/or Characteristics.**

When Detective Logan said, "Somebody shot Winterbourne," the word "somebody" was a placeholder standing for the as yet unknown killer and "shot Winterbourne" was a known Characteristic of the murderer. By using the placeholder "somebody," Logan could express the cause-effect relationship in a simple sentence that was easy to hold in his mind and think about.

Other placeholders we use every day are "someone" or "something" for unknown Things, "something about" for unknown Characteristics, and "somehow" for unknown causes. For example:

> "Someone (an unknown human Thing) left the cap off the toothpaste."

> "Something (an unknown Thing) really stinks in here."

> "Something about (an unknown Characteristic of) his sales pitch sounds too good to be true."

> "Somehow (an unknown cause) he got an "A" in History without ever reading the textbook."

While these "some" words are the usual placeholders, you can use any crazy thing that stands for an unknown Thing, Characteristic, cause, or effect. In his book, *Secrets from an Inventor's Notebook*, Maurice Kanbar describes how he and his partner Al Kolvites come up with their inventions using their own unique placeholder.

> In the early stages of your product development, after you've pinpointed a problem and while you are brainstorming solutions, you might use a stand-in substance. Al calls it "nonexisteum." Nonexisteum is infinitely light, infinitely strong and costs nothing. With it, you are free to be very creative and your plans proceed beautifully. But at some point you have to get real and find an existing substance that will meet your designs demands. What kind of adhesive will withstand high temperatures? Which materials resist rust? What kind of fastener will keep manufacturing costs down? What will make this game safe for children? That's when it helps to know how things are made and how they work.[5]

Observe that Kanbar begins by naming "nonexisteum" as the Thing that solves his problem. Once he has that, he can focus on his Purpose (inventing a new adhesive, material, fastener, or children's game) and the Characteristics of his as yet unknown Thing (withstanding high temperatures, resisting rust, low cost, or safety).

Hypothesizing

Once you're clear about your Purpose and what Things, Characteristics, causes, and/or effects you're looking for, your next step is making a guess about what the missing "somethings" and "somehows" might be.

This is what scientists call "hypothesizing," but what it really boils down to is *intelligent* guessing. A proper hypothesis is a guess that includes all the information you already have and contradicts none of it.

Why did Joey's balls roll? He could have guessed that the shape had something to do with it because all his balls looked the same, shape-wise, and they all rolled. A bad guess would be that a relevant Characteristic was being red. Joey's red ball rolled, but so did his blue one, so saying something had to be red to roll contradicted a fact Joey already knew.

Who killed Winterbourne? Logan guessed at the killer's Characteristics and assumed it was someone who had entered and exited through the window, used the gun found underneath the fire escape, and had a motive for killing the victim. A bad guess would be that Winterbourne committed suicide, since shooting yourself in the back five times is rather hard to do.

How do you come up with a good guess about what the missing placeholders might be?

Isolating Characteristics from Things

If you know at least one Thing related to the effect you want to understand, it means that it necessarily has **some** characteristics or properties that caused the effect. In other words, some characteristics of that particular thing are causal Characteristics, so take a close look at the thing and pay attention to its characteristics. Ask yourself which of those might be required to cause the effect.

Joey already knew that balls are Things that roll, but what about them – what Characteristics – made them do that? He observed some of their attributes: their size, shape, color, weight, location, smell, etc. He guessed that it might be the shape.

Logan was also guided by his observations and what he already knew when he hypothesized about what the murderer's Characteristics might be. The killer had the Characteristics of being in the room at the time of the crime, not entering through to front door, and not being able to walk through walls, so it was a good guess that he entered through the open fire escape window.

He guessed that the gun they found under the fire escape was the murder weapon because it was so close to the probable escape route and it's rare to find a gun just left lying on the sidewalk. If that was the gun used in the murder, it would have to have certain Characteristics such as being able to shoot bullets of the same caliber as the ones found in Winterbourne's body. When it shot those bullets, there would be marks on the bullet casings that were unique to the gun that fired it. Would they match the markings of the bullets in the body?

Was the killing an accident? Hardly. If someone had been shot once it might have been an accident, but five times? No way! That meant that one of the murderer's Characteristics was that he had a *motive* for shooting the victim.

So all of Logan's guesses and assumptions were based on Characteristics he knew the killer possessed.

Comparing characteristics of different things

One way to come up with a good guess as to what the Characteristics might be is to compare different, but similar, things. Do the Things that act or change in the way you want to explain have any common characteristics? Do the things that don't act that way lack those same characteristics? If so, one or more of those common characteristics are likely to be the necessary Characteristics you're looking for.

In Joey's case, he wanted to know why some things rolled and some things didn't so he compared a little red and a big blue ball (same shape, different color and size) with each other, a red ball with a red block (same color and size, different shape), and a ball (always rolls) with a soup can (rolls on the label side but not on the top and bottom).

Reality Testing

Once you have a good guess as to what the Things and/or Characteristics you seek might be, your next step is to test your hypothesis and see what happens. A Reality Test is a process of using similar things keeping as many things and characteristics the same *except* for the things or characteristics you think might cause the effect. If you do that, then whether or not the effect happens is a good test of whether you chose the right thing or characteristic.

Let's see what Joey did and what he was thinking. We'll watch as he compares things and their characteristics, observes similarities and differences, makes guesses, performs Reality Tests on his guesses, and finally discovers why balls roll.

He pushes a little red ball.

Wow! That thing really moves! What else can I push?

He pushes a little red block.

That wasn't as much fun. It hardly moved. How come? What's different? They're the same size, so that's not it. They're the same color, so that's not it. They're not the same shape. Maybe that's it. I'll push something else. What else looks like this ball?

He pushes a big blue ball.

*This rolls too! It's bigger than the little red ball, but it rolls. It's blue, not red, but it still rolls. I guess the size and color don't matter. Is it the ball shape? Does anything else roll that's **not** ball-shaped? How about this soup can?*

He tries to roll a soup can.

It rolls on the side with the label. It doesn't roll on the top or the bottom. Why?

He looks at the top of the soup can, picks up a block, and compares the two.

The can is flat on the top and bottom. It doesn't roll on the top or bottom. The block is flat on all sides. It doesn't roll on any side. The can does roll, but where it's "not-flat." Are balls flat anywhere?

He inspects the two balls.

*They're "not-flat" everywhere! Round means not-flat. Round things roll. Flat things don't roll. Round things roll **because** they're "not-flat." Balls roll **because** they're "not-flat" – or round – everywhere.*

He looks for and tries rolling other flat and round things just to see if it always happens.

Joey has learned, not only that balls roll, but **why** they roll. That might seem rather obvious and trivial, but it's knowledge Joey will use many times in his life: at seven when he learns how to bowl, at 18 when he gets a flat tire, and at 32 when he sits on the floor with Joey Jr. and shows him how to roll balls and soup cans.

What Joey did is, in principle, exactly what scientists do. They seek causes, make guesses (hypothesize) as to what the causes might be, and then Reality Test their guesses by running experiments.

When scientists run an experiment, they compare things that have the properties they think might be necessary Characteristics with others that are the same except that they don't have those properties. For instance, they may give pills with a new medicine to one group of patients and similar pills without the medicine to a similar group of patients to see if the medicine makes any difference.

How to find causes step by step

Here it is, as easy as 1, 2, 3, 4, 5.

1. Have a clear Purpose.

The most common reason people fail to find causes is that they don't have, or are unclear about, what their Purpose is. That's why, if your thinking is muddled, confused, or going nowhere, defining your Purpose is your first order of business.

Since having a Purpose means wanting to find out something you don't already know, the best way to state that fact clearly is in the form of a question.

"Who killed Winterbourne?"

"Why do the balls roll and the blocks don't?"

"What is the best way to get to Chicago?"

"Where can I find a good doctor?"

"How can I afford a new car?"

"When should I leave to avoid rush hour traffic?"

Once you state your Purpose in one simple question, it will clarify and focus your thinking and set you up for the next steps in answering your question.

2. Identify what you know.

If something happened you can't explain, start with what you already know. You know **that** it happened. You know what things it happened with or to and these could be Things. Examine their characteristics because whatever properties you can identify might be Characteristics.

If your goal is to make something specific happen, you know a great deal about **what** you want to occur in the future and the Things and Characteristics that might be involved even if you don't know how to do it yet. Note what the known things are.

3. Use placeholders for what you don't know.

State the answer to your question using placeholders for what you don't know.

"Somebody killed Winterbourne."

"Something about the balls makes them roll."

"Some way is the best way to get to Chicago."

"Somewhere I can find a good doctor."

"Somehow I can I afford a new car."

"I should leave sometime before the rush hour."

4. Hypothesize.

Make an intelligent guess as to what the unknown Things and/or Characteristics might be, using what you already know.

5. Reality Test.

Test similar things, some which have the property you think might be a Characteristic and some which lack that particular property, to see if the effect still happens. If you find that something is a Thing that causes the effect, check to see if similar things have the same effect.

That's the general order of what you do to find a cause, but you may not go straight through from Step 1 to Step 5. If your hypothesis fails to pass the Reality Test in Step 5, you'll have to go back to Step 4 and come up with a new guess. If you find that you don't even know enough to make a good guess, then you need to go back to Step 2 and gather more information.

If all goes well, you'll eventually find the cause you're looking for. When you do, can you really be sure you've got it? Sometimes. You'll see when and how in the next chapter.

CHAPTER 5

Are you sure you know the cause?

Once you come to a conclusion or think you know something, how sure are you? How sure do you need to be? If you've decided you might like seeing a certain movie and it turns out to be awful, the worst thing that happens is that you've wasted a little time and money. But if it involves something serious like investing your life savings or getting married, it matters a lot. With the important issues in your life, you not only need to have a pretty good idea about what to do, but you need to be as certain as you can be that you're getting it right. Sometimes, it's a matter of life and death.

Reasonable doubts

"All the prosecution has is circumstantial evidence," defense attorney Terry Payson told the jury when Sherman Wilson was brought to trial for the murder of Nelson Winterbourne. "Wilson was framed."

Payson recalled the prosecution's handwriting expert to the stand.

"You've testified that Winterbourne's signature was forged on these checks. Since they are in such large amounts, they also had to be signed by Mr. Wilson. What did you conclude about Wilson's signature?"

"They're forgeries too."

Payson called the bookkeeper, Mona Hanes, as his next witness.

"You were employed by Winterbourne & Wilson?"

"For eighteen years," she replied.

"You set up the books and had access to all the customer accounts?"

"I did."

"Do you have a key to Mr. Wilson's office?"

"Of course. He travels a lot and keeps valuable things in there. When he's away and I need something, I just go in and get it."

Payson nodded and smiled. "He trusted you." Drawing closer, he casually asked, "So what were you doing on Winterbourne's fire escape the night of the murder?"

"What?"

Payson then entered into evidence a security video taken about the time of the murder from the bank at the corner of Allen and Fifth Street. It showed a slender female taking off a big dark coat and a baseball cap, putting them into the trunk of a Ford sedan, and driving away.

Payson presented close-ups of the person taking off the coat and cap to the jury. "Sure looks like you, Ms. Haynes. And you own a Ford sedan?"

"That wasn't me!"

"I would like to enter into evidence this close-up of the license plate of the car driving away from the bank. Is that your license plate Ms. Haynes?"

"I don't have to answer that."

"The murderer was wearing Mr. Wilson's coat and hat, and used the gun he kept in his desk at work, but drove your car, and has your face. How do you explain that?"

"I don't have to answer. I want a lawyer."

"The defense rests."

The wrong cause

If the prosecution thought they had a good case against Sherman Wilson, they were wrong–but that's not unusual. Mistakes and errors happen to us all the time. A homeowner may think he knows how to replace a faucet but, instead, he causes a flood and has to call in a plumber to rescue him. Two friends disagree about something and each one is so sure that they make a sizable bet about it–and one of them loses.

Then again, a person can actually come to the right conclusion, but if he isn't *sure* he's right, he won't have the confidence to act on it. A young man who's afraid he might be wrong may not invest in the stock that could make him a millionaire or propose to the woman of his dreams.

Knowing if you're right or wrong can be a big deal. So is being able to tell the difference between being absolutely, dead-bang certain and having a strong gut feel that something is probably true, but not being totally sure about it. What you need is a Certainty Test to determine if you're right and, fortunately, there is one, but let's begin by asking why people get things wrong.

The wrong view of causality

People often get cause and effect wrong, as we saw in Chapter 2, because they have a wrong view of causality. They assume it means one thing happening after another or correlation or action and reaction. Let's revisit those examples of flawed reasoning and see why, if you understand causes in terms of the Characteristics of Things, you won't make those particular mistakes.

> With a decrease in the wearing of hats, there has been an increase in gasoline consumption over the same period.
>
> Conclusion: Gasoline consumption is caused by people abandoning the practice of wearing hats.

There aren't any Characteristics of hats (the Things) that cause an increase in gasoline sales.

> As ice cream sales increase, the rate of drowning deaths increases sharply.
>
> Conclusion: Ice cream consumption causes drowning.

What Characteristics of ice cream cause drowning? None. Does the increase in ice cream consumption have any Characteristics in common with swimmers drowning? They both happen in the summer. Why? Both eating ice cream and swimming are things people do to cope with summer heat.

> The more firemen fighting a fire, the bigger the fire is observed to be.
>
> Conclusion: Firemen cause an increase in the size of a fire.

What Characteristics of firemen (the Things) make the fire bigger? There aren't any. If you then switch it around, you'll see that a big fire (the Thing) has the Characteristic of requiring more firemen to put it out.

Insufficient Information

If you study the Things and Characteristics that are relevant to your Purpose, you'll learn a lot about what *probably* caused the effect you want to understand. Do you know enough to be sure? Maybe not.

You may know which Things act or change and what some of their characteristics are, but even if you know that those characteristics have always been present when the effect occurs, is that all you need to know to conclude that they're the Things and Characteristics you want? No, because correlation isn't causation.

Even if you do know for sure that something *is* a Characteristic – like a Thing has to be round to roll – all that means is that the Characteristic is **necessary**, but not that it's **sufficient**. If it's not round it won't roll, but just being round doesn't mean that it *will*. It won't roll if it's made of a non-solid material or you're trying to roll it on the wrong kind of surface. There may be additional Characteristics and Things required that you don't know about yet.

Sometimes you know the Characteristics, but there's not enough information to identify the Thing. Logan was sure that the murderer used the fire escape and the gun they found was the murder weapon. He had a good guess as to the identity of the killer, but he still didn't have enough evidence to be certain, beyond a reasonable doubt, that Wilson did it.

When it can't be true

The sure sign you made a mistake is when you end up with a contradiction. It might be that you suppose something exists that doesn't, like when you think you have enough eggs to make a pound cake and you open the refrigerator to find only one egg. What you see contradicts what you thought was there.

What is a contradiction? Aristotle's Law of Non-Contradiction states: "It is impossible that the same thing belong and not belong to the same thing at the same time and in the same respect."[6] Putting that into Thing/Characteristic language, it means that a Thing cannot both have and not have the same Characteristic at the same time and in the same respect. Your fridge cannot, at the same point in time, both contain and not contain enough eggs to make a pound cake.

There's a contradiction when what someone thinks, or supposes, or expects doesn't match the way things are in the real world. If a carpenter thinks he cut the shelf to exactly the right length, but it doesn't fit, he made a mistake. If a traveler goes south to reach a destination that's actually to the north, he won't get there because he's going in the wrong direction.

The **Error Test** is:

IF YOU FIND A CONTRADICTION, YOU CAN BE SURE THERE IS AN ERROR.

Applying the Error Test to the murder case, if Wilson was on the fire escape, wearing a black coat and a red baseball cap, and went north toward Fifth and Allen Street, then the person who arrived there soon after in that coat and cap should have looked like Wilson – but she didn't. She looked like the bookkeeper instead – which contradicted the prosecution's allegation.

It is or it isn't

In the real world there aren't any contradictions. Everything is what it is and isn't what it isn't. Things have the Characteristics that they have and not the Characteristics they don't have – and that's all. There is no in-between having and not having a particular Characteristic. That was Aristotle's Law of Excluded Middle.[7]

But is that right? You can probably think of plenty of "middles." Something may be black or white and, then again, it might be gray. Someone could be tall or short or in between those extremes and just be average in height. That's not a problem.

In the black-white-gray example, Aristotle would say that something is either black or not-black, white or not-white. The gray would be both not-white and not-black until it got so dark that you'd have to call it black or so light that it would be white. Black, white, and gray mean **ranges** of a characteristic. For those Characteristics that denote ranges, the Characteristic is either within the range or it's not within that range. There is no other "middle" possibility.

If you understand that contradictions cannot exist (the Law of Non-Contradiction) and that a Thing either has or doesn't have a given Characteristic (the Law of Excluded Middle), that will lead you to knowing when something **is** true and **has to be true**.

When it has to be true

If we find a contradiction in someone's thinking, it means he made an error. He believed that a Thing had a Characteristic it really didn't have. The truth would be to state that the Thing has a Characteristic that it actually does have.

The way Aristotle put it is: "To say of what is that it is not, or of what is not that it is, is false ..." In other words, if you have a contradiction, then you know it's false. He continued "while to say of what is that it is, and of what is not that it is not, is true ..."[8] That means that if you say that something is what it is or isn't what it isn't, then your statement has to be true.

It's true that something is what it is and has to be what it is, otherwise it would be a contradiction. It has to be true because it cannot be otherwise. That's the Law of Identity: that things are what they are and A is A. It's true that the light is on if the light is on or that if something is not a circle, it's not a circle.

So what? Any statement in the form "A is A" is trivially true. The really interesting statements – the ones that philosophers have been arguing about for centuries – are in the form "A is B" like "All men are mortal." How can you know and be sure that *this* is true? By looking at the WHYS.

Why a statement is true

Why are all men mortal? Why do men die?

We know that all men have certain biological characteristics in common with all other men (and all higher animals). We are composed of cells which can die, malfunction, become infected, or turn cancerous. Our bodies consist of complex interrelated systems – circulatory, respiratory, neurological, endocrine, etc. – and these have vital, irreplaceable components like the heart, lungs, brain, etc. If any of these systems fail or their key components malfunction, a man will die. Sooner or later, even if we can avoid accidents and survive diseases, some vital organs **will** fail because they wear out with time and use.

Observe that the answer to "Why do men die?" – as it is for all causes – is found by identifying the relevant Things and Characteristics. In this case, the Things are the human body and its vital organs and their Characteristics are that, over time, they wear out and can no longer function properly and keep the body alive. All men (who have bodies that eventually wear out, malfunction, and cannot keep them alive) are mortal (have bodies that eventually wear out, malfunction, and cannot keep them alive).

Is that so?

At this point you might object. What happens if we can alter human bodies so that they don't wear out any more? Then "All men are mortal" might become false. Actually, it wouldn't.

A man whose body doesn't wear out – let's call him Man 2.0 – is different from what every man is now (Man 1.0). They're not exactly the same kind of Thing, so while all Man 1.0's are mortal, all Man 2.0's might not be.

If two things share many common characteristics, but don't share the particular Characteristics necessary to produce a given effect, the effect may not happen. If a red wooden block and a red wooden ball are identical in every respect except shape, just because the ball rolls doesn't mean the block will. If Man 1.0 is mortal, it doesn't mean that Man 2.0 is.

On the day that Man 2.0 does appear on the scene, it may become necessary to specify that when you say "All men are mortal" you mean Man 1.0 only. That's why, whenever you're trying to find a cause, it's a good idea to clearly and precisely define your terms whenever you refer to a class of things ("all men") or to identify the specific thing ("Joe Jones") that you're referring to. That way you know what you're talking about and, when you do find the cause you're looking for, you'll know which Things your explanation applies to and which it doesn't.

Causes turn "A is B" into "A is A"

We asked why all men are mortal – the Characteristics that make every Thing that is a man eventually die – and we identified the cause as having a body that wears out. Knowing that was the reason, we could restate an "A is B" statement:

> All men (A) are mortal (B).

into an "A is A" statement:

> All men (who have bodies that eventually wear out, malfunction, and cannot keep them alive) are mortal (have bodies that eventually wear out, malfunction, and cannot keep them alive).

Substituting "A" for "have bodies that eventually wear out, malfunction, and cannot keep them alive" we get:

> All men (who are A) are mortal (A).

When we know the specific Characteristics of A that **cause** B, it converts an "A is B" statement into an "A is A" statement that **has to be true**. You can be absolutely certain of it.

The Certainty Test

We saw that any statement in the form "A is A" is true and has to be true. We can also be certain of something like "All men are mortal" if you can find the cause that converts it into the form "A is A."

The **Certainty Test** is:

IF YOU IDENTIFY THE CAUSE THAT CONVERTS AN "A IS B" STATEMENT INTO AN "A IS A" STATEMENT, YOU CAN BE CERTAIN THAT "A IS B" IS TRUE.

Let's see how this works with another example.

All calico cats (cats with white, black, and orange fur) we had observed had been female, but we didn't know why. As a result, we couldn't say, with confidence, that calico cats are **always** female because someday we might find a male calico.

After studying feline genetics, scientists discovered that calico coloring occurred when a cat had certain specific genes on each of **two** X chromosomes. If a cat had a required gene on one X chromosome only, it would be white, black, and gray rather than white, black, and orange. Since all males have one X chromosome and one Y chromosome (XY) while females have two X's (XX), only females had white, black, and orange fur.

Knowing the genetic cause, let's try the Certainty Test. We restate the "A is B" statement:

> Calico cats (A) are females (B).

as an "A is A" statement:

> Calico cats (who have two X chromosomes with certain genes) are females (have two X chromosomes).

Substituting "A" for "two X chromosomes" we get:

> Calico cats (who have A with certain genes) are females (have A).

Since having two X chromosomes causes calico coloring, it explains why we never saw any male calicos.

That was fine until the day that *Mr.* Calico showed up. Now what? If we were so sure that the previous genetic explanation was true, how could we account for this creature?

When scientists examined the unusual cat's genotype, they discovered that it was neither female (XX) *nor* truly male (XY). While it appeared to be a male, it had an extra sex chromosome and was actually XXY, a condition known as Klinefelter's syndrome. Thus, calico color still required two XX chromosomes and the old explanation still applied, but it applied to more than just female cats.

Carrying over causal knowledge from one situation to another is very common – and extremely useful. Finding the cause that explains one type of thing often provides insight into the characteristics and actions of other Things that have the same Characteristics. If we know why all men are mortal, the same biological characteristics explain why all dogs and cats are mortal too.

Seeking certainty

Sometimes finding the cause that satisfies the Certainty Test can be easy. All it may take is one observation to identify the causal Characteristics and know that you've got it. But often the cause-finding process is difficult and time-consuming. A biologist might dedicate his entire life and run thousands of experiments seeking the cause of a disease and never discover it.

Some causes are impossible to determine with certainty because of the nature of the Things you're dealing with. Trying to understand people is a case in point. You cannot know, for sure, why other people do what they do because you're not a mind-reader. You can't get inside their heads and directly observe the thinking that causes their actions. All you can know for sure is what you see them say and do, but you can only guess as to why.

It's also impossible to know with absolute and total certainty what happened when you weren't around. Did John Wilkes Booth assassinate Lincoln? It's extremely probable because, if it were untrue, it would contradict so many things you know, but you can't be as sure of it as you can about what you're seeing with your own eyes right now.

Nonetheless, you often have to act on incomplete and uncertain knowledge. So what do you do? You do the best you can and continue to look for causes using the process described in Chapter 4.

When you identify what is known and unknown, there are always some pieces to the puzzle you can be sure of. While the police didn't know who murdered Winterbourne, they knew with certainty that he was dead. They knew that the gun they found under the fire escape was almost certainly the murder weapon because, when they fired it, the spent bullets had exactly the same unique markings as the ones in the victim's body.

As for the unknowns, even if you don't know the cause with absolute certainty, when you use the correct method, you'll be getting closer and closer to it. You may not learn everything you want to know, but with each step on the road to truth you'll understand more and more and be able to act with greater effectiveness and self-confidence.

All along the way you'll be acquiring important information about what the cause might be. Your best guesses – your hypotheses – will be better for it. Then your Reality Testing will weed out false assumptions and logical dead ends.

It's said that Thomas Edison made more than a thousand attempts to make a long-lasting light bulb. They were all unsuccessful because the bulbs never stayed lit for more than a few minutes. When one of Edison's colleagues asked him, "Mr. Edison, don't you feel you are a failure?" he answered, "Not at all. Now, I definitely know more than a thousand ways how NOT to make a light bulb."

Did Edison have to do a thousand experiments before he got a working light bulb? Maybe not. We are all born with special abilities we can use to make cause-finding much easier. In the next chapter you'll find out how to "data mine" your huge built-in Database to get information in an instant and the chapter after that will show you how to use your emotions, first impressions, and gut feelings to identify and achieve the things that are most important to you.

Data Mining

Gathering information used to be a time-consuming and difficult task involving trips to the library, finding reference books, consulting experts, etc. Now it's much easier. You can locate exactly the facts you want easily and quickly just by typing a few key words into a search box. But no internet search can access the most important Database of all – yours.

Your Database has everything you've ever experienced and done, everyone you know, everything you desire and aspire to, every thought you've ever had, and everything you like and don't like from every hour, minute, and second of your entire life. But, if you're like most people, you can't get to most of that information when you want to. Fortunately, there's a fast and easy WHYS Way to access your own Database too. Let's see how.

Lou and Jenn's night out

Lou had been looking forward to this day for a long time. The last of his of six children was fully launched with a job and a place of her own and now, after thirty years of living with kids, it was just him and Jenn again. This afternoon he had traded in "The Whale," their oversized gray minibus, for the two-seater Italian sports car he had his eye on for years. He called his wife from the dealer to say "Wear something nice tonight, Jenn-Jenn. I'm taking you out to Il Mulino in my new car."

As they drove to the restaurant, an old song came on the radio. "That was playing on your boom box the day I first saw you at the beach," Lou said. "There you were soaking up the sun in a blue and green bathing suit with your long, sun-streaked hair and gorgeous legs. I just had to talk to you, but instead, I ..." Lou then launched into an impassioned rendition of the song on the radio, just as he had on the day he met Jenn.

"I'm surprised you still remember the words. I haven't heard that song for years!" she said.

"Neither have I," Lou grinned, "But I don't forget things like that."

Over dinner Lou reminisced. "I knew you were the one for me on our first date when we went to that movie with Doris Day and what's-his-name and we both laughed in all the same places." They had a lovely meal and when the check came, Lou calculated the tip, paid, and they left.

Lou glanced out over the parking lot – and panicked. Where was "The Whale?" Did someone steal it? Then he realized that he now had a new sports car that wasn't big and easy to spot among the other cars and that he had better begin to pay attention to where he parked it. "Where'd I park the car, Jenn?"

"It's two rows to the right of the entrance," she said heading toward that aisle, "and half-way down just before the boulder."

She was right. It was right by the big rock. As they approached the car, Lou exclaimed, "Rock Hudson! That's who was in the movie with Doris Day."

How did Lou recall what his wife was wearing the day he met her? How did the lyrics of that old song get into his head and stay there for thirty years? Why did his wife know where he parked the car when Lou didn't? Why did Lou suddenly remember the name "Rock Hudson?"

Remembering names and numbers

"I hate history!" said Robb to his friend Jack. "I'm not smart like you and I can't force all those names and dates into my head. They just fall out. How do you remember all that stuff?"

Instead of replying, Jack asked, "Who's the best hitter on the Lancers?"

"Definitely David Weiskopf – at least for now. He's hitting .343, but Juan Esposito is a close second at .330. He's especially good against right-handed pitching and the Lancers will see a lot of that on their next road trip. And don't rule out Norm Bellis. He's only batting .250, but he hit .322 last year and he's the best base-runner and fielder in the league. The season's still young and I expect Coach Berry will keep him in the line-up and he'll have a chance to pull up his batting average.'"

"For a guy who can't remember names and numbers, you're pretty good when it comes to baseball," observed Jack.

Your Database

As Lou was enjoying dinner with Jenn, he wasn't thinking about arithmetic, but when the check came, the math facts he learned in elementary school were right there when he needed to figure out the tip. Where did they come from? Where did Robb get the latest batting averages when Jack asked him?

They came from their personal **Databases**. Everyone has one. You have one. It's where everything you know is stored.

It holds a huge amount of information. Just think about all the movies and TV shows you've ever seen. If someone mentions one of them, you could probably recall what the story line was, who some of the actors were, whether or not you liked the characters they played, etc. Like Lou, you know the lyrics to songs – perhaps thousands of songs – including the words to that annoying commercial you just can't get out of your head.

Sometimes it's very easy to get to your knowledge. Lou had no trouble at all recalling the words to the song he sang to Jenn or how to calculate a 20% tip. Robb had the latest Lancer batting averages on the tip of his tongue. Yet sometimes you can't remember or struggle to retrieve things you think you know or ought to know like Lou who, at first, drew a blank on the name "Rock Hudson" or Robb who stared at the history test and couldn't recall the dates of the Civil War.

Your Database has trillions of facts that you might want to access and "data mine," but to make the most of it, you need to know how your Database works and the best way to get information into and out of it.

Data entry

Everything stashed in your Database first got there in one of two ways: sense perception or introspection.

All of your knowledge of the external world begins with information that comes through your five senses: vision, hearing, touch, smell, and taste. That's sense perception and it's the way you make contact with everything outside of your own body. Introspection is how you become aware of things going on inside yourself. It's how you know that you're hungry or thirsty or tired and the way you learn that dropping a brick on your toe hurts. In the next chapter, we'll discuss introspection in much greater detail, but now let's look at how sense perception works.

When you first perceive an apple, you become aware of the whole thing and not just the sensations of red and solid and in-your-hand. In other words, you perceive the whole **Thing**. After you perceive something, you can focus on its individual sensory qualities, but you originally experience it as an entire Thing.

Data storage

Once you perceive something with your senses, what happens to the information? How is it stored? That varies a lot from person to person and a good analogy might be how Lou stored things in his garage before and after he got his new car.

The garage

Lou had no intention of parking his sports car on the street and exposing it to the elements and other hazards, but their garage was so full of cruddy junk and a thirty years' accumulation of God-knows-what that even a small car wouldn't fit in what was supposed to be a two-car garage. How did all that stuff get in there anyway? It just happened.

When Jenn's family came to visit for Thanksgiving 22 years ago, Lou cleared out the guest room for them. He took the cartons that were still unpacked from their last move, piles of outgrown toys and clothes, some unused furniture, and other things cluttering up the guest room and put them against the wall in the garage. A few years later, he threw the leftover carpeting from redecorating the living room on top of the boxes and the other items from the guest room. Over the years, the garage filled up.

Data organizing

If you don't do anything special, your Database will fill up like Lou's garage but the process isn't totally random. There is some automatic organizing going on.

For example, the items added more recently, like the extra carpeting, were easier to get to than the unpacked moving boxes from the guest room underneath. In your Database, things you experienced more recently are easier to remember than things that happened to you long ago because old information tends to get buried under new data.

Also, items you've used recently are easier to find. Lou knew exactly where the bicycles were because he and Jenn rode them to the park at least once a week. Similarly, Lou easily recalled the arithmetic he learned in second grade because he used it almost every day, but he would be hard pressed to tell you all the state capitals which he memorized in the same grade.

Association

Another principle is that items from the same time and place tend to become associated with one another. The items Lou took out of the guest room were in the same place against the garage wall. Likewise, everything he perceived on the day he met Jenn – the beach, the weather, the song, what she looked like, what she wore – were associated with each other and stored in the same place in his mental Database. When he recalled the song, everything connected with that day came to mind.

Importance

The main reason why the day Lou met Jenn was so easy to remember is that when something is very important – if it's associated with strong feelings like desire, happiness, fear or loss – it makes a stronger imprint. It puts a bold sign with big letters and flashing lights on certain experiences and on everything associated with them. That's why you remember where you were when you first heard about a significant historical event or the death of someone close to you and it's why, even years later, you can remember such things better than most of what you did last week.

Robb was such a passionate fan of the Lancers that their activities had a special place in his life and thoughts. Everything the Lancers did made a strong impression on him. "The reason why history is so easy for me" his friend Jack explained, "is that I want my teams to win in history just like you want the Lancers to win.

"History is all about conflicts between people. It's about wars and elections and issues and Good Guys versus Bad Guys. In any historical period, I pick the side I think is right and support it against its enemies. In the American Revolution, I wanted the Founding Fathers to beat King George III. Slavery is evil, so when we studied the Civil War, the Union was my 'home team' and I rooted for them against the Confederacy."

The bottom line is that Jack **cared** about what happened in history, but Robb didn't and just wanted to pass the next exam. Jack had a **personally important reason** for wanting to know historical facts and Robb didn't. Jack did well in history and Robb didn't. Here again, we see that having a personal Purpose not only motivates, guides, and empowers thinking, but is also important for successful data storage and Data Mining.

Conscious organizing

Data storage by association and importance happen automatically, but there are a few things you can do on purpose to store your knowledge in a way that makes it much easier to get to.

Bookmarking

Bookmarking consists of deliberately associating what you want to remember with other Things and is especially useful for short-term recall.

Jenn remembered where Lou parked the car because she bookmarked it. Since her yellow subcompact – "The Goldfish" – wasn't visible above other cars like "The Whale" was, she always consciously noted its location by reference to two stationary Things – in this case, the restaurant entrance and the boulder. As they walked from the new car to the restaurant, she pictured returning to it by leaving the restaurant, turning right to the second aisle, turning left down the aisle and continuing on until she saw the rock.

Many memory experts like Harry Lorayne have systems based on picturing and associating Things. For instance, Lorayne remembers names by associating a person's facial features with a picture that reminds him of the name.

> Look, you've just met Mr. Crane. A picture of a large crane, as used by construction workers, comes to mind; or perhaps the storklike bird. You've looked at his face and decided that

his high forehead is the outstanding feature. You look at that forehead, and *really* picture many large cranes flying out of it; or, you can see them attacking that large forehead! Or perhaps the entire forehead is one gigantic crane. As with any association, you have many choices as to the kind of picture you visualize. You must be sure – *force* it at first – to really see that picture. The next time you meet Mr. Crane, *you'll know his name!*[9]

Bookmarking is fine for things you don't need to remember beyond a day or so like a parking spot or a shopping list, but for long-term storage, there's a better way.

Organizing by Characteristics

Lou welcomed Jenn's help in cleaning out the garage. She was the family organizer and could always locate anything in a flash. When Sally presented them with their granddaughter Vanessa, Jenn dug into the box she labeled "Sally's pictures" and made a collage of Sally's baby pictures as a present. She also found the embroidered pink baby blanket that once kept Sally warm and would now be Vanessa's.

Jenn began the cleanup by asking Lou to go through the items in the garage and sort them into one of three groups based on the Characteristic of what he wanted to do with each item: throw it out, give it away, or keep it. After disposing of the things they didn't want, they looked at the "keepers" and grouped them into categories based on common Characteristics like what they were used for or who they belonged to like sporting goods, holiday items, car stuff, cleaning things, Jenn's miscellaneous, Lou's miscellaneous, and uncategorized. Then they took everything out of the garage, cleaned the floors and walls, and installed floor-to-ceiling shelving around the perimeter. They filled the shelves putting the golf clubs, fishing poles, and baseball bats together, the Christmas tree near the outdoor lights and the wrapping paper, etc. When they were done, they could easily locate anything and there was plenty of room to park Lou's new car – and the "The Goldfish," too.

Automatic Data Mining

The secret of successful Data Mining is to make the most of the automatic functions of your mind. Once you have a Purpose – something you want

to know or do–the Data Mining will begin all by itself. When you need
to add two numbers, the rules of arithmetic will come to you.

After you begin the process, it will continue without any additional
effort on your part until your Purpose is satisfied. That's how Lou finally
remembered "Rock Hudson" after initially drawing a blank on the actor's
name. He wanted to say the name, but couldn't remember it, so he let it
go and went on to do and think about other things. Meanwhile, the Data
Miner in his brain kept digging for the answer without any more effort
on Lou's part. Then, when he saw the rock in the parking lot, it triggered
an association with Rock Hudson's name.

Data Mining your own Database is like searching for something on the
internet. You type what you want into the search box, an automatic
process begins, and, if all goes well, you find it. In Data Mining your
Purpose is the "keyword" you use and then you "hit enter" and let your
mental "search engine" take over from there.

That sounds pretty simple, doesn't it? Just ask for what you want and
you automatically get it. So why doesn't that always work?

Missing Data

No matter how hard Robb tried to remember certain historical facts
during an exam, he couldn't. He hadn't read the textbook and he wasn't
paying attention in class. He couldn't pull the facts out of his Database
because they were never there to begin with.

Data organization

If you don't do anything to consciously organize your knowledge, things
will accumulate haphazardly in your Database like they did in Lou and
Jenn's garage. Then it will be tough to locate what you want.

Just last spring Lou spent hours looking for some baseballs, gave up,
and bought new ones. This year, he went right to the shelf and, next to
the big carton with the basketball and soccer balls, he found a shoebox
labeled "Baseballs," opened it up, and there they were.

If you have a well-organized physical space, you can quickly get what
you want when you want it. Data Mining works that way too. If you've

stored your knowledge properly, your Database will work efficiently and remembering what you want will be effortless and automatic.

Importance

When Lou recalled his first date with Jenn, the name of Doris Day's co-star wasn't important to what he wanted to tell her. What he most wanted to say was that's when he knew he was in love with her and that wasn't hard to remember at all.

Search keys

When you search for something on the internet, if you don't put the right key words into the search box, it will be much harder to get what you want.

Let's say you just heard a song for the first time today and you liked the female singer's voice, the lush violins in the background, and the words "soft blue petals falling." Which key words would most likely find you that song?

1. Love song

2. girl +violins

3. song +lyric +"soft blue petals falling"

Yes, number 3 is the best choice. Why? Because it is **specific**.

Number 1 isn't very good because there are thousands and thousands of love songs, and the second search would probably just get you a list of young female violinists. Only the last one zeroes in on the Characteristics that are most **unique** to the **particular** song you heard.

It's also like that with Data Mining because having a good search key is critical. Fortunately, you have your Purpose and the clearer and more specific you can be about what you want to dig out of your Database, the more likely you are to find it. For example, if you're deciding what to do after work, you'll be likelier to get a good result if your Purpose is to try out a new restaurant than if you don't have a Purpose or it's something nonspecific like "Do something that's not boring."

Automating

Lou could easily recall how to calculate a 20% tip because he did it so often. If you do something over and over, it becomes automatic. That's how we form habits and, in general, that's a very good thing. It saves us having to recall or relearn how to walk across a room without falling over, whether to reach right or left to get the salt shaker when cooking, etc. It's a time and labor-saving feature built into our mental equipment.

Sometimes, however, it's not so good. When circumstances change, automated thinking can give you the wrong answer or get you into a mental rut. That's what happened to Lou when he looked for his car in the parking lot. Thousands of times before, all he had to do was scan the lot and he could see the roof of "The Whale" above all the other cars – but this time it wasn't there.

Trying too hard

When you're Data Mining, setting your Purpose is the conscious part, but then you have to let the actual search go on automatically after that. If you deliberately try to control or force it, it won't work. If you tell yourself, "I've **got** to remember this," you'll fail, probably feel stupid, or begin wondering if you're getting Alzheimer's. As we'll see in the next chapter, unsuccessfully trying to force an automatic process is a perfect set-up for anxiety and self-doubt.

Data Mining step by step

Let's put all this together into the essential steps for successfully and efficiently unearthing the treasures in your Database.

1. Store by Characteristics.

As you go through life seeing and doing things, **pay attention to WHY** certain things suit your Purposes. Why do you like plaid shirts? Why is the little vise-grip perfect for opening a bottle of soda?

Note the relevant Characteristics that make them suitable, useful, and of value. For instance, the little vise-grip, unlike the big one, is small enough to fit into the kitchen tool drawer next to the refrigerator so it's right there when you take out the soda.

Once you identify essential Characteristics, the built-in processes of memory and association will take over and your knowledge and experiences will be automatically stored by Characteristics for efficient retrieval.

2. Reorganize as necessary.

That's fine advice going forward, but what if you've rarely paid attention to the important Characteristics of things and your Database is as full of disorganized junk as Lou's garage? No problem. It's never too late to tidy things up.

Most of the time the automatic "last learned, last used, and associated" automatic data storage system is good enough, but if you're trying to find an answer without success, ask "Why?" and focus on Characteristics.

Imagine you want to put an expensive art poster above the fireplace in the living room, but how? All you can think of is taping it to the wall. That won't work. Why? Because tape will mar the poster and would be tacky in your formal living room. You're also worried about heat and smoke rising up out of the fireplace. Why? That could damage the poster, too. You need to hang it in a way that will protect the poster (Characteristic) and look good in the room (Characteristic). Then you know what to do. You get a poster frame with the same wooden finish as the arms on the sofa and a non-glare glass on top.

3. Search purposely and specifically.

The clearer you can be about what you want to get out of your Database, the more likely you are to get it. Think about what you want and why you want it then home in on the **specific** Characteristics that it needs to have.

4. Use Standing Orders.

Once you focus on what you want, your internal Data Miner will get busy finding it for you – but maybe not right away. If the information is buried deep or tangled up with irrelevant associations, it could take a while to dig it out.

One thing that will help is setting a Standing Order. That's a request for your Data Miner to be on the lookout for the missing information and that's how Lou eventually remembered "Rock Hudson." Lou set a Standing Order using "what's-his-name" as a placeholder for the information he was trying to recall.

5. Relax!

Follow steps 1–4 and that's all you have to do. If the information is in your Database or you encounter it later on, your Data Miner will eventually find it. Let go and let it happen.

CHAPTER 7

WHYS emotions

All day long – and even at night in dreams and nightmares – you feel emotions like desire, fear, joy, sadness, pride, guilt, satisfaction, frustration, love, and hatred. Where do these reactions, "intuitions," "instincts," and "gut feelings" come from?

Your emotions make you want to act – to get some things and avoid or get rid of other things – but should you? Should you go after everything you want and avoid anything that feels scary or risky? Can you trust your feelings to tell you what to do?

And what about emotional conflicts? How can you resolve them? What do you do with love-hate relationships? How should you act when you have mixed feelings?

To find the answers, let's explore what emotions are, why we have them, and how they work. You'll see why, no matter how complex, incomprehensible, and irrational emotions may *seem* to be, once you grasp a few simple, basic principles about them, they make sense. You'll see why emotions are necessary for your happiness and you'll learn how to decode, evaluate, and use the vital messages they contain to live a successful, meaningful, and fulfilling life.

Hiring a manager

The Accounting Manager was leaving to have a baby and Dean needed to hire her replacement. Erika Bauer, his first of two candidates, had an impressive resume and reference letters that extolled her competence and reliability.

"How do you do, Mrs. Bauer," he greeted the neatly-dressed middle-aged woman, "Tell me something about yourself." The minute she began to speak, he was shocked at his own reaction. He hated her.

It wasn't what she said – she said she had just moved to town with her husband and was interested in the job – so why did he feel that way? What about her did he hate so much?

She spoke with a German accent and there was something about that he didn't like, but there was more. It had to do with the way she looked.

She wore reading glasses that hung from a silver chain around her neck and seeing them, Dean felt anger and dread. Why? Who did he know who wore glasses on a chain like that? And then he remembered Mrs. Klemmacher.

Mrs. Klemmacher, the lady next door when he was growing up, was evil. She was always yelling at the neighborhood kids and making up things about them. Dean never forgave her for telling his mother that she had caught him deliberately tearing down her front yard fence when he hadn't gone anywhere near her damn fence. His mother believed it and punished Dean by not letting him go on the scout trip he'd been looking forward to for months.

Mrs. Klemmacher spoke with a German accent and wore glasses on a chain. She had a stocky build like Mrs. Bauer, too.

So what?

While the lady asking for the job looked and acted so much like that horrid neighbor that it was scary, she was **not** Mrs. Klemmacher. Besides, there was nothing inherently evil about being stocky or German or wearing reading glasses on a chain. Dean realized that, his anger disappeared, and he went on with the interview.

Dean didn't have such a dramatic initial response to the second candidate, Marvin Graf, but the more he spoke to him, the more uneasy he felt about letting this man anywhere near his company's finances. Why?

For one thing, Graf didn't look him in the eye. Perhaps he was just a shy person and it didn't mean all that much, but it seemed as if Graf were somewhere else other than in the conversation. His eyes wandered around the room, only occasionally focusing on Dean – but seldom on his face – as if sizing things up for some purpose.

Something else besides Graf's eyes were evasive. When Dean asked "Why did you leave your last job?" the man didn't really answer the question but, instead, spouted vague generalities about the business climate and theoretical psychology. Dean was now very uncomfortable and feeling, "I don't trust this guy."

The alarm bells went off loud and clear when Graf proudly told how he had under-reported a previous employer's expenses on a loan application and deceived the bank into giving his boss a loan he otherwise didn't qualify for.

"If you could put one over on the bank like that, how can I be sure you'd be straight with me?" Dean asked.

"You can't be sure," said Graf with a conspiratorial smile, "but if you pay well, it buys a lot of loyalty."

Dean decided to hire Mrs. Bauer.

Why did Mrs. Bauer make such a strong negative first impression? Could Dean trust his emotions? Considering his reactions to the two job applicants, did Dean do the right thing? Why?

The therapist

From what Brian's parents had told Dr. Weiss, the fifteen-year-old fidgeting in the chair, was a fine boy, decent and smart, and the therapist wanted to help him.

"Your Mom and Dad say you used to be pretty happy, but something's changed. They tell me you've always been a straight-A student and now your grades are dropping. They see you moping around the house, never going out, silent at dinner, and they're worried about you. Should they be?"

"I guess."

Weiss nodded. "Life is tough at your age: a lot of pressures and changes, school, people you can't always trust, friends, girls ..."

When the therapist mentioned girls, Brian's eyes widened, and then, as if a switch were thrown, his face became completely blank.

"What do you think of girls?" Weiss casually inquired.

"I don't want to think about them."

After a few sessions, it was clear that the trouble began two months ago when Brian asked pretty Mallory Jones for a date and she turned him down announcing loudly so that all his friends could hear, "I wouldn't be caught dead in public with a nerd like you."

Brian tried to push the pain of being rejected out of his mind by denying what he was feeling. When that didn't work, he began avoiding girls and thinking about girls or anything that reminded him of girls, and also anybody who might think he was a nerd.

Dr. Weiss was worried that Brian's "I don't want to think about it" attitude could turn a real but manageable problem into a serious neurosis. The boy needed to learn about, feel, and think about his emotions rather than push them aside. The therapist was confident he could help.

Brian hadn't yet built thick walls of repression and other defenses to cope with painful feelings of loss, anxiety, and guilt. If Weiss intervened now, he could show Brian how to understand and manage his emotions. That would set him on the right path and keep him from turning out like 35-year-old engineer Spencer Woods.

Spencer originally came to see Dr. Weiss with an anger management problem. He was prone to sudden, unexplained rages that frightened everyone – especially Spencer himself – but other than that, he felt nothing. The engineer never smiled, even when Weiss cracked a joke or paid him a compliment. Nothing made Spencer happy, nothing made him sad, nothing was particularly important to him – and he liked it that way. Sitting stiffly straight, he announced proudly "I am always rational and never emotional."

"Except for your temper," Weiss pointed out.

Over the last year, the therapist had been helping Spencer dismantle his neurotic defenses and showing him how to reconcile reason and emotion. They were making progress but it hadn't been easy and Spencer still had a long way to go.

Is repressing emotions a bad thing? What else can you do with horrible feelings like pain, guilt, and fear?

Where emotions come from

Emotions don't just come and hit you from out of nowhere although it may feel that way at times. They start with your experiences, past and present, the same as everything else you know. What you feel now is a response to things and events in the present, but it depends on memories from the past stored in your Database.

The most important information kept in your Database is your knowledge of what has been good for you and bad for you, what has led to success or failure, and what has been pleasurable or painful. Emotions connect your memories with the built-in pleasure/pain system that we human beings share with other animals.

Your present perceptions, actions, and thoughts automatically and constantly trigger feelings and emotions like desire, joy, fear, guilt, frustration, etc. telling you in an instant whether what you're perceiving, doing, or thinking about is good or bad based on your knowledge of all the things that ever happened to you and whether they were associated with good or bad outcomes.

The biological function of your feelings is to guide you toward the things you need and away from others that threaten you, and to motivate you to take the actions your well-being requires. That's why, as we saw in the last chapter, emotionally charged experiences make a stronger imprint and are easy to remember. In fact, you don't have to Data Mine and seek out what was good for you or bad for you in the past. It comes after *you* and tries to tell you what you should do right now. That's what emotions are for.

There are two basic kinds of emotions: ones like happiness, joy, and satisfaction that feel good and others like fear, pain, and guilt that feel bad.

Feel Good Emotions

Some feelings steer you **toward** certain things. These are **motivating** emotions. Your Purposes – the values and goals that motivate you to act – always start with wants and desires. For instance, if you're running on a hot day, you may become dehydrated, feel thirsty, and want a drink of water.

When you finally do gulp down a nice cold one, it satisfies your desire and it feels really good. So does achieving **any** goal or Purpose you want whether it's earning an "A" in English, marrying the love of your life, or just getting something simple and ordinary like a good parking spot at the mall.

While desires are motivating, other Feel Good Emotions like happiness, joy, and satisfaction are **rewards** for actually achieving something you wanted. They make you glad that you did what you did and that makes you want to keep on doing it so you can feel good again.

Feel Bad Emotions

Some emotions don't feel good at all. Who likes to feel guilty or frustrated or wants to experience pain or anxiety? Yet unpleasant and negative feelings serve an important and, sometimes literally, life-saving function. Feeling pain is the way you become aware that something is going wrong and needs attention.

Physical pain tells you that some part of your body is injured or malfunctioning while psychological pain comes from losing something that you wanted to get and/or keep. What you lost could be the blue ribbon you wanted but didn't win or the favorite vase that fell off the table and shattered. Any loss of something you want or need is painful and the more significant the lost thing is, the greater the pain. The more sudden the loss is, the more intense the pain.

Since living well depends on gaining and keeping what you want, you try to avoid losses and the pain that comes from loss. That's why it's good that you have Feel Bad Emotions. They're your built-in "alarm system" that warns you when trouble is coming or when you might be in danger.

If you're walking down a stair and your foot slips on the step, you might experience a sudden panicked fear of falling and, before you even have time to think, you lunge for the handrail, grab it, and regain your balance. Being afraid was a good thing because the fear prompted you to act and save yourself from falling.

Likewise, just contemplating doing something you shouldn't do could give you twinges of guilt. If that's what keeps you from saying something hurtful to a friend or downing the extra slice of pizza that blows your diet, it was a good thing that you felt guilty. Even when it's too late and you realize that you actually did something you shouldn't have, being ashamed of yourself can motivate you to think about what you did wrong so that maybe you won't do it again next time.

What emotions are trying to tell you

Whenever you feel an emotion, it's because something in the present has triggered an association with some past experience or event that was good for you or bad for you. Your reaction is sending you a message that something going on right now could be important, valuable, and/ or dangerous.

But simply feeling an emotion isn't usually enough to get the full message. It's very easy to miss it, misread it, or not know how to translate it into words you can grasp and evaluate.

Dean's reaction to Mrs. Bauer – "This woman is evil and will hurt me" – was triggered by her being a stocky woman with a German accent, wearing glasses on a chain – all characteristics associated in his memory with Mrs. Klemmacher. Dean's initial "I don't trust this guy" uneasiness with Graf also came from his encounters with indirect and evasive people who later proved to be dishonest. His emotions were sending him messages in both cases, but could he trust them? Are past associations relevant to the present?

They might or might not be and the only way to know for sure is to put your feelings into words, and then analyze and Reality Test their messages. When Dean did that, he saw that there were additional reasons to mistrust Graf but that his first impression of Mrs. Bauer was way off base.

Translating Feel Good Emotions into words

Translating motivating or rewarding positive emotions into words is rather easy for most people. A desire for X means "X is good. Go for it." The feeling of happiness you get when you achieve what you want says "Good for you for getting X. You did it. Keep up the good work."

Translating Feel Bad Emotions into words

When you experience painful and unpleasant emotions – when you feel depressed, anxious, afraid, frustrated, angry, ashamed, etc., – what can you do about it besides feeling rotten? The next step – and the best way to get control of the situation – is to translate the feeling into words which, for Feel Bad Emotions, can often be very difficult.

Translation is much easier when you understand that each *type* of emotion contains a particular, unique message. Just as Feel Good Emotions communicate ideas like "Go for it" or "Good for you," Feel Bad Emotions do too. Each feeling corresponds to a sentence that's a formula for that particular emotion. Then, once you can state what your emotions mean in words, you can think about them, evaluate them, and get a handle on them.

Pain

Pain means "I have lost (something of value)." It's what Dean felt as a child when his mother wouldn't let him go on the scout trip. It's what Brian felt when Mallory rejected him. In Dean's case the lost value was the trip he was looking forward to and, for Brian, it was the date with Mallory and the hope that she would find him attractive.

How much pain someone feels depends on how important the value is to him. That's why Dean was crushed when he couldn't go on the trip but only slightly bothered when the dog ate one of his socks.

Fear

Fear means "I am in danger of losing (something of value)." It's your basic "alarm system" warning emotion.

The intensity of the fear varies with the importance of the thing you value and with the immediacy of the threat. Fear can range from a "Something's not quite right here" gut feel that Dean had when he began the interview with Graf to a soldier under fire realizing that he is about to die.

Frustration

Frustration means "(An obstacle) is preventing me from achieving (a goal)." It's what you feel when you need to get to an important appointment by 10 am (the goal), but it's 9:55 and you're stuck in traffic (the obstacle).

Anger and hatred

Anger means "(Someone) has done me an injustice." It's closely associated with hatred which means "I want to stop or punish (someone) who has destroyed or threatens (something I value)."

Lee gets angry when people talk during a movie or play and it's not just because he can't hear the dialog. He takes such rudeness *personally*. He thinks it's insensitive and unfair for someone to annoy *him* like that. In fact, he hates it so much that he's been known to kick the offender's seat and tell him to shut up.

Self-esteem emotions

Anxiety and **guilt** are the most common, and the most important, Feel Bad Emotions. That's because the value at stake is **you**, your whole self, and your view and estimate of yourself. The value is your self-esteem.

There are two parts of self-esteem. The first part is what you think of your **ability** to get what you want out of life. Are you good at achieving your goals and getting things done? Are you smart enough? Do you have the skills? Are you a winner or a loser?

The second part is your estimate of your **worth** as a human being. Are you a good or bad person? Do you do what you should do? Have you done bad things and are you likely to do them again? Are you a hero or a jerk?

To have self-esteem is to feel "I am an **able and worthy** human being." No value, except perhaps for life itself, is more important than self-esteem.

People with high self-esteem face life with optimism and confidence, take on risks, and work to overcome difficulties with the certainty that they **can** do it and they **deserve** the rewards. Those with self-doubts avoid risks and challenges and abandon activities when the going gets rough. They don't think they have what it takes to get what they want and and/or they don't really deserve to get it even if they could.

Anxiety

Anxiety is a special kind of fear about the part of self-esteem that involves your **ability** to deal with and control the important issues in your life.

The one-sentence formula for anxiety is: "I've got to (do something) and I can't." Anxiety is the fear that you'll be **unable** to do something you must do. It impacts self-esteem because it says you're not good enough.

Brian's anxiety about girls fit the formula exactly. Being a biologically normal fifteen-year-old male, he had a strong attraction to females he saw every day, but after his devastating encounter with Mallory, he was afraid he wasn't the kind of person a girl would like. For Brian it was "I've got to get a girl to like me, and I can't."

Coping with anxiety–the right way

The best way to deal with anxiety is to first identify the feeling's message and then Reality Test the message to see whether it's true or not.

Dr. Weiss guided Brian through the process.

"Mallory doesn't like you, but she isn't the only girl in the world. Do *all* girls feel that way? Nah! Believe it or not, some girls actually prefer "nerds" and think smart guys are sexy. ... Yeah, I know. You're clumsy and ill at ease around girls. That's a fact. But is that really a permanent condition? An intelligent young man like you can *learn* social skills. I've got some books here for you on how to do it. Once you know what to do, you can practice in real situations with real girls until you get the hang of it. ... Yes, that's scary, but do it anyway. You'll probably screw up and make a fool of yourself a few times, but you won't die. "

Eventually, Brian gained control of his anxiety when he saw that he could find some wonderful girls who appreciated quiet, honest "brainiacs" like himself, and that by using his new social skills, he *could* interact with them successfully. "I've got to make it with girls and I can't" became "I want to get a girlfriend and I can."

Coping with anxiety–the wrong way

Since Feel Bad Emotions like anxiety are there to alert us and keep us from getting hurt, why don't more people understand their messages and heed their warnings?

The main reason is that experiencing feelings of anxiety -- from a constant, wearying, self-doubt to sudden terror and panic -- can be extremely hard to bear. When that happens, some people view the anxiety itself as the threat and then they do all kinds of things to try to avoid feeling it. They may use substances like drugs or alcohol to deaden the pain or they may engage in compulsive behaviors to distract themselves from thoughts or perceptions that trigger Feel Bad Emotions. It's as if the building is on fire, a fire alarm is going off, and the watchman, annoyed that the loud noise is hurting his ears, simply shuts off the siren and ignores it.

That's how Spencer got to the state where he hardly felt anything at all. Growing up, he had suffered abuse from both his parents, lived in constant fear of them, and was helpless to do anything about it. He coped by ignoring his feelings, and then situations or thoughts that might arouse those feelings or any emotions at all, until it became a habit which psychologists call repression. It took Dr. Weiss months to find this out because, when he asked the engineer about his childhood, Spencer reported that he couldn't remember anything. His life before he left home at 18 was a blank.

Although Spencer ignored his emotions and the abuse which caused them, that didn't make them go away. The pain kept festering in his soul. Over the years, Spencer had adopted additional defense mechanisms like a distorted self-image ("I am always rational and never emotional.") in an attempt to reinforce the walls of repression when his dammed up feelings threatened to break out and overwhelm him. That didn't work either. When they did break out, he lost control and flew into a rage without a clue as to where it was coming from.

Guilt

Guilt or shame relates to the part of self-esteem that has to do with whether you're a good and **worthy** person.

The one-sentence formula for guilt is "I shouldn't do (an action) but I did or will." It's what you feel when there's a conflict between your moral standards – with what you consider right and good – and your actions.

Whether or not someone will feel ashamed depends on both his actions and what his moral standards actually are. For instance, a Mafia hit-man can kill three people in a single day and not feel the slightest guilt because, to him, the right thing to do is to get rid of his boss's enemies. Also, some people suffer from unearned guilt over things they didn't actually do and had no choice about like feeling guilty about surviving a catastrophe they were in no way responsible for when other people perished.

Coping with guilt–the right way

In addition to social anxiety with girls, Brian also suffered from unearned guilt. He resented Mallory and wanted revenge, but he told himself that he shouldn't feel that way. He should be more tolerant and forgiving.

Dr. Weiss set him straight. "Never feel guilty about what you feel. There are no evil feelings. There are only evil deeds." He explained that emotions are automatic, unchosen reactions conveying information from past experiences and that's *all* they are. Feeling certain emotions doesn't make someone a bad person as long as he doesn't do bad things. He showed Brian how to deal with guilt by analyzing and Reality Testing both his actions and his moral standards.

"Sure, you'd like to get even with Mallory. That's because she hurt you and she's a shallow and cruel person. What's not to hate? As for tolerance, what would happen to you or to the world if everyone tolerated hurtful, cruel people? Maybe tolerance isn't all it's cracked up to be."

After that Reality Test, Brian's "I shouldn't dislike her that much but I do" became "I have a good reason to despise her and I do." The guilt vanished when he realized it was perfectly OK to *feel* all kinds of "evil" things as long as he didn't actually *do* something that was wrong.

Coping with guilt–the wrong way

When someone feels guilty, he should think about his actions and the moral standards that caused the feeling, but people often don't. Guilt is such a painful emotion that people have come up with dozens of neurotic defenses to fend it off such as:

Denial – "I didn't do anything wrong."

Rationalization – "I flunked the test because I had a lousy teacher."

False self-image – "So I get welfare checks, sponge off friends, won't get a job, and spend all day at the beach. That's what a great surfer like me does."

Projection – "Nobody's 100% honest. Everybody cheats."

Emotional conflicts

As we've seen, your feelings are constantly sending you messages that urge you to do certain things, and most of the time, you do. Gene felt hungry around noon and he wanted a sandwich. He ate a sandwich. No problem. But what do you do when your emotions are giving you mixed messages?

When Gene's dear friend Sid wanted to borrow some money, Gene was pulled in two different directions. Part of him said, "Sure, help Sid" and another part said "Don't do it!" Gene had a problem.

That's when he needed to identify the messages causing his conflicting emotions and to Reality Test them. On one hand, Gene wanted to help Sid because he was a sweet guy, they had so many good times together, and Sid had always stood by him. On the other hand, Sid was careless with money and didn't always keep his promises. The odds were good that Sid would never pay him back. Gene didn't mind losing the money, but the unpaid debt would bother him and hang over their relationship.

Once Gene understood the causes of his conflict, he could see his way to resolving it. "I wish I could lend you the money," he told Sid, "but I'm afraid I can't. "

You can use the same process Gene used with *any* emotional conflict. It works especially well with the crucial self-esteem Feel Bad Emotions of anxiety and guilt since both are emotional conflicts. Anxiety is a clash between "I've got to" and "I can't" and guilt is a conflict between "I shouldn't" and "I did."

First identify the specifics of the conflict. What is the "I've got to," the "I can't," the "I shouldn't," and/or the "I did?" Then Reality Test.

If you're anxious, ask some questions. Do you really have to? Are there other ways to get what you want? Are you sure you can't? Is there any way you can change things so that you can?

If you feel guilty ask: Why *should* you have done something? Why was it bad that you didn't? How come you didn't do the "right" thing? Was there something about the action that didn't seem right? Did the "right" thing threaten or conflict with something else you wanted more? If you discover that one of the conflicting messages is false or irrelevant to the current situation, that often resolves the conflict immediately.

At other times, the problem is a clash of *desires*. You want two things – and they're both good things – but you can't have them both. You can't spend the same evening at the theater and with friends who just came in from out of town. If that's the case, you've got more thinking to do. You have to decide which of the competing desires is more important to you and why. Once you do that, you'll know what to do.

WHYS emotions step by step

Emotions are your friends. They can guide you, encourage you, and warn you of danger. In a split second they can access your entire Database of past experiences and calculate the net sum – for good of for bad – of all the things that are similar to what you're facing right now. They are powerful tools for living a happy and successful life – but only if used properly.

Here's how to do it.

1. Feel the feeling.

This seems obvious because your emotions can't do anything for you if you won't even acknowledge their existence. Sad to say, people don't pay enough attention to what they are feeling for a variety of reasons.

Sometimes it just hurts too much. While Feel Bad Emotions are often hard to bear, ignoring them doesn't make them go away. It only cuts a person off from the information their emotions are trying to give them about losses and potential threats.

Sometimes a person mistakenly believes that there are things that good people should or should not want, hate, fear, etc. In fact, "shoulds" don't apply to emotions at all. Right and wrong is a matter of choices and we can't choose our feelings.

When your reaction to something seems wrong or makes no sense as Dean's did with Mrs. Bauer or Brian's to Mallory, it doesn't mean that you're a bad person. All it conveys is that you're responding automatically to something from your past, which may or may not be right, true, or relevant to the present. Determining whether it is, requires a Reality Test – which you're less likely to perform if you moralize, feel guilty about, or deny what you feel.

2. Put the feeling into words.

If the feeling could talk, what would it say? Free associate a little. Is it "I hate _____," or "I want _____," or "I've got to _____," or ...? If you get stuck, but can identify the general feeling, use the one-sentence formula for that emotion and fill in the blanks. For instance, if you're feeling guilty, the formula would be, "I shouldn't _____, but I did." So ask yourself what you did that you shouldn't have done.

3. Identify the triggering Things and Characteristics.

Finding the cause of a feeling is exactly the same as finding any other cause. You identify the relevant Things and Characteristics.

What *characteristics* of the thing you're responding to make you feel the way you do? For Dean, the cause of his reaction to Mrs. Bauer was her accent, wearing her reading glasses on a chain, and being middle-aged and stocky. What other person had those Characteristics? Mrs. Klemmacher! She was the cause of his reaction.

4. Identify the action.

Your emotions impel you to **do** things like pursue what you desire, avoid a danger, stop doing something, etc. What action is the feeling urging you to take?

5. Reality Test the message.

Once you know what the feeling is trying to tell you, you may need to evaluate it to see whether it's true or relevant to your current situation. Generally, it's all right to act on and enjoy Feel Good Emotions without further analysis, but not always. If it involves an important matter with long-term consequences, like choosing a career or buying a house, don't simply act on impulse. Give it more thought. Also, if you have mixed feelings or even a hint of "Maybe I shouldn't," the matter needs further scrutiny.

Needless to say, Feel Bad Emotions *always* need a Reality Test. The entire reason those feelings are there is to interrupt your life to tell you that something has or may go wrong. Pay attention! Their message may be a warning you should heed and then again it might be a false alarm, but the only way you'll know for sure is to Reality Test it.

6. Reality Test the action.

If you have time to think about what your feelings are urging you to do, consider the possible effects. Although Brian wished Mallory ill – and justifiably so – he wasn't going to kill her or even spread malicious gossip about her. He thought better of it after realizing what the consequences might be.

7. Get help when necessary.

All the above steps are what you *should* do, but you may not be able to on your own. If you're in the grip of extremely painful or overwhelming emotions, it can be hard to think straight. The pain may be more than you can bear. With complex or mixed emotions, you may have difficulty translating your feelings into words or unearthing the past experiences that triggered your reactions.

Sometimes all you may need to put things into perspective and regain control is talking it over with a family member or empathetic friend. It's worth a try. If that doesn't work or you're still having trouble getting in touch with your feelings or putting them into words, seek professional help.

Look for someone who practices Cognitive Behavioral Therapy (CBT), the school of therapy originated by Aaron Beck (http://www.beckinstitute .org). Here's a description of their approach:

> [CBT] is a short-term, goal-oriented psychotherapy treatment that takes a hands-on, practical approach to problem-solving. Its goal is to change patterns of thinking or behavior that are behind people's difficulties, and so change the way they feel. It is used to help treat a wide range of issues in a person's life, from sleeping difficulties or relationship problems, to drug and alcohol abuse or anxiety and depression. CBT works by changing people's attitudes and their behavior by focusing on the thoughts, images, beliefs and attitudes that we hold

(our cognitive processes) and how this relates to the way we behave, as a way of dealing with emotional problems.[10]

A good CBT therapist can help you connect with and identify your emotions, understand their underlying messages, and help you root out and overcome negative and self-defeating thinking habits – often in only a few sessions or a few months.

Having emotions is good for you. They're motivating, rewarding, and can alert you to what is important or dangerous. But they can also mislead you, so you should not be impulsive or act on whim. Instead, if you regard your feelings as *data* for thought, look for their causes, and Reality Test them, you'll benefit from your emotions and be in control of your life.

CHAPTER 8

Achieving goals

What do you really want? Will you ever get it? You can if you go after your goals *The WHYS Way*. What about the big things that seem so difficult and daunting like writing a book, building your dream house, or becoming an MD? You can achieve your demanding long-range goals the very same way you accomplish simple everyday things like making breakfast or getting to work on time. Let's see how.

Scrambled eggs

"Can you make me scrambled eggs, Grandma?" asked six-year-old Lisa.

"How would *you* like to make them? You're old enough to cook real food on a real stove and I'm going to show you how," said Grandma as she took out her cookbook and opened to the page with the recipe.

"It says you should get four eggs, ¼ cup of milk, 2 tablespoons of butter, and salt and pepper." Lisa got the ingredients and put them on the counter by the stove.

"Next you need to get a mixing bowl, my wire whisk, a measuring cup for the milk, and a frying pan to cook the eggs in." Lisa got them too.

"Now what do we do? Do we put the eggs in the frying pan and cook them?" Grandma asked as she took an egg, still in the shell, and placed it into the frying pan. Lisa giggled.

"You gotta take the shell off!"

"Right you are," said Grandma. "I'll show you how to do the first one and you can do the rest." After all the egg yolks and whites were in the mixing bowl, Grandma said, "We could cook them now, but then we'd have sunny-side up eggs."

"The scrambled eggs hafta be scrambled."

Grandma handed Lisa the whisk saying, "And you're the Scrambler-in-Chief."

After Lisa blended the eggs until they were a nice lemony color and measured and added the milk and the salt and pepper, Grandma showed

Lisa how to turn on the stove, melt the butter in the frying pan, and cook the eggs. Then Lisa put half the eggs on one plate for Grandma and the rest on her own plate, briefly admired her handiwork, and ate them with gusto.

Why was making the eggs a multi-step process? Why did the order of the steps matter?

The morning rush

Monday through Friday Nick would get out of bed, shave, shower, dress, get breakfast, and be in his car on the way to work in 23 minutes flat. He didn't waste a second. He didn't stop to read his email or make his bed. Those could wait until after work.

Saturday was a different story. He got out of bed when he felt good and ready. Unshaven and still in his pajamas, he ambled downstairs into the kitchen and, instead of gulping down milk straight out of the carton and grabbing a granola bar to eat in the car, he decided to make pancakes, bacon and coffee. When he was done, the phone rang. He could have let it go to voicemail, but he picked up the phone to chat with his brother. When Nick hung up an hour later, his breakfast – cold pancakes, cold bacon, and cold coffee – was waiting for him. As he popped everything into the microwave he thought about how sweet it was to not have any goals or deadlines, and be able to kick back and play it by ear this morning.

Why was Nick so focused and efficient on weekdays, but not on Saturday?

The Project Manager

Kate commanded high consulting fees as a Project Manager because of her reputation for designing and building large-scale, high-quality computer systems and completing them on time and on budget.

When she was hired by a shipbuilding firm, her job was to build a huge, complex system to automate the design and manufacturing of aircraft carriers and military cargo ships. She headed a project team that consisted of six programmers, an expert on manufacturing software, and a database expert and she had six months and $2 million to do it.

First she interviewed the users of the new system to find out what they required and then she wrote the specifications. From the specs she developed a project plan that broke down the entire project into the tasks and sub-tasks that needed to be accomplished and in what order. Then she made an estimate of how long and how much it would cost to complete the system and it seemed doable within her budget and timeframe. Her estimate included extra time and money in accordance with her "Two Major Disasters Rule." She knew that in any large-scale project she could expect one or two unforeseen – but totally devastating – problems and she needed to allow for enough time and resources to deal with them.

Kate made a 16-foot long wall chart of the project showing all the tasks and their places on a time line. Each team member had a color. When they began a task, they outlined the task box on the wall chart in their color and, when they completed the task, they colored in the whole box. When all the tasks up to a certain point were complete, Kate advanced the time line with a thick black marker – and a great deal of ceremony – at the Friday morning status meeting. Kate's rule was that if the project was on or ahead of schedule, the whole team would celebrate with a two-hour lunch after the meeting. The team member who was most ahead on the chart picked the restaurant and got a free lunch too.

Kate was always available and ready to help her team members do their assigned tasks. Her friendly, casual style made it easy for a team member stuck with a problem to come to her, and she got them unstuck. But mostly, *she* came to *them*, wandering around from desk to desk to see what they were up to, letting her team members know that she appreciated their efforts and why, and offering suggestions. She was always in control of the project and didn't have to wait until Friday morning to find out how everyone was doing.

As she expected, problems occurred and not everything went according to plan but, nonetheless, the project was finished on schedule. The shipbuilders loved using the new system and the team members had such a great time, they were sorry to see the project end.

What did Kate do that made her such a successful project manager and how can you apply that to getting the big things *you* want done?

What are goals?

A goal is either getting something you want or doing something you want to do. Lisa's goal was to have scrambled eggs, Nick's weekday goal was to get to work on time, and Kate's was to deliver a well-functioning and thoroughly debugged computer system on time and on budget.

Cause and Effect

So how do you get from where you are now, with your objective not yet reached, to where you want to be with your mission accomplished? Understanding cause and effect is the key.

You need to take actions *now* that will **cause** you to achieve your goal in the *future*. Your actions are the cause, accomplishing your goal is the effect, and the three main causal components – your Purpose, Things, and their Characteristics – are essential.

Achieving your goal is your Purpose, but what are the Things and Characteristics? That depends on what your goal is. For Lisa, the goal and desired effect was yummy scrambled eggs that she made all by herself. The Things she needed were the ingredients and the kitchen tools she used to change the eggs from being raw, cold eggs in their shells into breakfast.

Nick required Things like a sharp razor, a warm shower, business attire, a carton of fresh milk, a granola bar, etc. Of course the basic Thing – the main thing that acted and/or changed – was Nick himself who, in 23 minutes, transformed himself from a guy sleeping in his PJs to a man dressed and ready to go to work.

Kate's goal was a well-functioning computer system and the Things she used were primarily *human* resources. Each person she worked with was an individual with unique Characteristics that could help or hinder the project. As we'll see in the next chapter, one of these people was responsible for Kate's first major disaster.

Ernie was the Naval Systems Division Manager and Kate's contact person. She made her weekly status reports to him and his function was to obtain computer and other resources for her. He introduced her to the system's users and found work space for Kate's team in an adjoining building. Other than that, he stayed out of her way and let her do her job.

The database and manufacturing experts were there to teach and share their knowledge with the rest of the team. All six programmers were bright, hardworking, and enthusiastic recent computer science graduates. They each knew several programming languages and had a good grasp of computer theory but, unfortunately, none of them knew the programming language to be used on the project. Kate immediately ordered six tutorial manuals and a set of reference guides which would arrive by next week when she would start teaching the programming language classes.

Tasks and sub-tasks

When master teacher Marva Collins' students were overwhelmed by the prospect of reading a thick book, she asked, "How do you eat an elephant?" The answer, "One bite at a time. You'll find that the process of achieving your goal is simply a series of steps and the secret of doing a big job is to cut the "elephant" into bite-sized pieces.

Each step or task should have its own goal. For making scrambled eggs that might be removing the eggshells and putting the yolks and whites into a bowl, adding milk, salt, and pepper, beating the yolks and whites together, etc. A task with its own goal makes everything more doable.

It takes what might be a daunting task and breaks it down into something more manageable. A task's goal also gives you something to go for that's closer and more immediately reachable than your ultimate goal and that can provide positive motivation along the way for getting it done. Most of all, as we saw in the last chapter, achieving any goal is pleasurable and satisfying. Lisa enjoyed her scrambled eggs, but she also took pride and satisfaction in her ability to crack the eggs into the bowl without making a mess. Having sub-goals provides more opportunities to feel good along the way to getting what you ultimately want.

The order of the steps

Can the steps be done in any order? Sometimes they can and sometimes they can't. Lisa had to remove the eggshells and blend the eggs and yolks before she could cook them, but the order of cracking open the individual eggs didn't matter. The order of the steps matters only when one step is **causally** related to another – and that's most of the time.

That's why cracking open and beating the eggs had to happen before cooking them. Eggs in their shells may be OK starting Things for cooking hard-boiled eggs, and an unbroken yolk is a required Thing for a sunny-side up egg, but they're the wrong Things for cooking a scrambled egg. Nick had to shower before he dressed for work, but whether he shaved before or after he got dressed didn't matter because shaving didn't (causally) depend on being dressed or not.

To determine the order of the steps, work backward from the final goal and identify the Things required and the sub-tasks that caused them.

For Lisa it was scrambled eggs
<caused by> cooking eggs
<caused by> beaten eggs
<caused by> beating eggs
<caused by> removing egg whites and yolks
<caused by> cracking open eggs.

Then list the steps from beginning to end.

Cracking open eggs
→removing eggs and yolks
→beating eggs
→beaten eggs
→cooking eggs
→scrambled eggs

Kate's project was very complex with thousands of steps that depended on each other in many different ways but the same principle of working backward from the final goal and ordering tasks according to their causal relationship to the final goal determined what had to be done before what. One of her many causal chains was:

Finish and test system
<caused by> writing individual programs in the programming language
<caused by> teaching programmers the programming language
<caused by> getting language tutorial manuals.

Therefore, one of the first things Kate had to do was to order the tutorial manuals because so much depended on that.

"Goals are dreams with a deadline."

If you don't have a deadline, what you want may never be more than a dream. If you have all the time in the world to do something, there's no urgency to do it and you'll be less motivated to do something *now* that will bring you closer to it.

That's why Nick was so efficient on work days. He knew within sixty seconds exactly when he had to be out of bed, shaved, out of the shower, and out the door. If he fell one minute behind, like on the morning his shirt ripped and he had to go get another, he skipped the milk and granola bar and put on an extra push to get out the door in time.

That may be one of the reasons why some tests of ability, such as IQ tests, are timed. Having limited time for a task can be motivating and energizing. Many people say that they work best under pressure and it tends to bring out their best performances.

Measuring progress

When reaching your goal involves a complicated, multi-step process over a period of time, you need to measure your progress so you can stay on schedule. You'll also know when you're falling behind in enough time to fix the problem and get back on track.

Measuring progress was the purpose of Nick's mental checklist and Kate's wall chart.

In his head, Nick had a list of his weekday morning tasks along with their respective deadlines. If he was going to leave the house at 8:23, he'd have to be in the kitchen to get the milk and granola bar by 8:21. The day he ripped his shirt, it was already 8:22 when he got downstairs, so he skipped breakfast.

Kate was responsible for the entire project and her wall chart gave her the necessary information she needed. The little colored boxes along the time line showed the current status of each sub-task and of the project as a whole. The chart also showed the individual team members how they were doing and their own contribution to the project. In addition, it often motivated them to increase their efforts. There was a friendly competition going between the two best programmers, Ray and Lucy. Both were running ahead of schedule, but Ray's last completed program was just a little farther along the timeline. Seeing that, Lucy decided to stay late and work through lunch on Thursday so she could finish her current program, edge out Ray, and get the free lunch on Friday.

Achieving goals step by step

Here's how to do it.

1. Make your goal as specific and as detailed as you can.

If you're not clear about what you should do, it may be because your goal isn't clear enough. That's often the case in the beginning of a project. What you need to do then is to specify your desired end result in greater detail.

When Kate came on the job, her goal was to build a computer system to control the manufacturing of ships, but that wasn't enough to work on. As she questioned and listened to the people who would use the new system, she filled in the details as to the expected results, the limitations and resources available to do it, etc.

2. Break the job down into tasks.

A big job is much less daunting and definitely more manageable if it's broken down into smaller tasks, each with its own goal. Gene Perret, who has written over forty books, observes:

> The task of authoring a complete book is daunting. In fact, it's formidable enough to scare many would-be authors away. Completing a book is a huge task and takes so much time, we tell ourselves, that it's hardly worth beginning. We continue to keep it as a long range goal in our minds, rather than converting it into a task that we can start right now.
>
> On the other hand, though, if we persuade ourselves to write only a small part of the book, we can start that tiny task and finish it *now*.[11]

List all the individual things that need to be done to get to your goal. If any of your listed tasks will take you more than a day or so to do, break it down into smaller tasks. For all but the smallest projects, estimate how long each task will take. This will be necessary for making your final plan.

3. Have a deadline.

Have a date and time by which you have to achieve your goal. This will motivate you to do your best.

Some goals have a built-in deadline such as Nick's need to get to work on time. Others don't. Nick's Uncle Damon's goal was to lose 15 pounds which he had been trying to do, unsuccessfully, for years.

Usually the best kind of deadlines to have are the ones imposed from the outside that involve a commitment to other people rather than just to yourself. Author Gene Perret reports that it was much easier to finish writing a book when he was given a cash advance on the condition he deliver the manuscript by a certain date. If he didn't get it to the publisher on time, he had to give the money back – but he'd already spent it.

If you don't have an external commitment, you can make one. When Uncle Damon quit smoking a few years back he told his family, friends, co-workers, and everybody he met that he was going to go "cold turkey" on his 50th birthday. He didn't want to let his family down or look like a fool in front of his friends, so he finally quit. Remembering how well it worked when he quit smoking, Uncle Damon decided to tell everyone he was going to lose 15 pounds by June 1st – the day his daughter was getting married. After that, when offered a scrumptious piece of cheesecake, he thought of his deadline, and opted for a piece of fruit instead.

4. Arrange the tasks in causal order.

Work backwards from your final goal. What task will finally cause the goal to be reached? What task is required to get to that task? Then lay out the tasks in causal order.

Break eggs → Beat eggs and yolks →

Cook eggs in frying pan → Eat eggs

Add butter to frying pan →

5. Add deadlines for each task.

For a large or complex project, once you have the tasks arranged in causal order, add your time estimates for each task from Step 3 to create deadlines for each task working backwards from your final goal. If Nick had to be out the door by 8:23 and it took two minutes to get breakfast, then his deadline for being in the kitchen was 8:21.

When estimating, follow Kate's "Two Major Disaster Rule." Add time for things to go wrong because you can always expect some unexpected problems.

Once you've laid out what has to be done, in what order and by what time, you've got your **plan.**

6. Measure your progress against your plan.

How are you doing? Are the tasks being completed? Are you meeting your deadlines?

When evaluating your progress, look back on what you've actually done so far rather than ahead to everything that's still left to do. Seeing how far you've come is more inspiring and empowering than despairing over how far you still have to go. Of course you should look ahead, but just focus on the next few tasks that need to be done according to your plan.

If you're falling behind or having other problems, how to handle that will be covered in the next chapter. The main point here is that when problems happen, if you've allowed extra time and resources for them, that shouldn't stop you.

To achieve your desires and dreams be clear about what you want, break the job down into manageable tasks, order them causally, set reasonable deadlines, make a plan, and go for it!

Solving problems

Problems, from little annoyances to major disasters, happen all the time and, most of the time, when something goes wrong you can you fix it using your knowledge of what worked in the past. But what do you do when you don't know what to do or when what worked for you before doesn't work now?

Let's see *The WHYS Way* to find, solve, avoid, and cope with problems.

The art class

"I give up. I can't draw."

The teacher approached eight-year-old Arnold's desk. "What's the matter?" she asked.

"I made it all wrong!"

"You don't like your drawing? Why?"

"It doesn't look like her at all," he said pointing to the seated girl posing for the class.

"Some of it looks like her," said the teacher. "What *part* of the drawing bothers you?"

"I made her head too big."

"I see. If you changed that would you like it better?" she asked handing Arnold a fresh sheet of paper.

He didn't answer. He just picked up his colored pencils and began drawing.

The missing manuals

Kate, the project manager, still didn't have the programming language tutorial manuals she had ordered for her programmers. They should have been delivered two weeks ago to Ernie, the Naval Systems Division Manager and Kate's contact person. Since Kate was working with her team in another building, she had been calling Ernie twice a day to see if they had arrived. She had stressed in her calls and her status reports that not having them was holding up the project.

Eventually, Kate decided to teach her programmers without them. Instead of the manuals, she printed out six copies of an actual program written in the programming language, one for each programmer, and used them to illustrate her lectures. In a week they were up to speed and coding like pros.

Debugging a program

"Oops, you've got a bug here," said Kate, circling a number on the Inventory Report that Nathan had programmed. "Six and four do not add up to twelve."

The programmer went back to his desk and spent an hour going over and over his program listing. When Kate came by to see how he was doing, he shrugged helplessly. "I've checked every single line of code and every one looks exactly right."

"Well, we know it can't be right, so let's reconstruct how we got twelve. Run your test again with a trace and every place that the total is used in your program, display its current value. Let's see if the displays show *where* in the program the total got messed up."

When Nathan ran his test, he discovered that when he first began adding up the numbers, the total already had a value of two in it. He hadn't zeroed out the total and the two was left over from totaling up the previous product.

The first major disaster

Kate was in the executive office building for a meeting so she stopped by Ernie's office. He wasn't there, but his assistant was. "Hi Susie. Did my tutorial manuals come in today?"

"Ernie got them two weeks ago."

"Does Ernie know that?" asked Kate.

"Oh, yes. He told me to put them in the janitor's closet."

Kate found them there. Why had Ernie been lying to her about something she told him was so crucial to the project?

A few days later, Kate returned from lunch to find her young programmers, a usually animated and talkative bunch, all silent and glum. "What happened?" Kate asked. Nathan looked down at the floor. Ray stared off into space. Finally, Lucy spoke up.

"Ernie was here. He said we're all a bunch of losers who don't know how to program and he's going to get us fired. "

"Damn that schmuck!" Kate cursed under her breath. Then she turned to her programmers. "Ernie's dead wrong. You're all terrific and I'm going to straighten this out right now."

Marching unannounced into Ernie's office, she confronted him. "You lied about having my tutorial manuals and today you abused my programmers. *What* are you doing?"

"Look, it wasn't my idea to have you do the shipbuilding system," he growled. "It should have been *my* project but for some reason they gave it to you and your bunch of stupid kids. Well, don't expect any help from me." Realizing further discussion was useless, Kate turned and headed down the hallway to the office of the Vice President. When he saw the look on her face, he asked what was wrong – and she told him.

"I'm not surprised," he said, shaking his head wearily. "Ernie's totally incompetent. We'd never trust him with an important project and that's why we brought you in to do it. The problem is, we can't fire him. We're a defense contractor and Ernie's father-in-law is a big shot in the Navy Department."

"I see. So what should I do?"

"Let's take Ernie out of the loop. Send your status reports to me and not to Ernie. If you have a problem or need anything, come directly to me."

"Will do."

"I'll make it clear that you're here to stay and that he is *not* to communicate with or interfere with your team in any way. I'll even change the entry code on your building so he can't get in."

That solved the "Ernie problem," but it had set the project back a week. Since Kate had planned for two major disasters and that was only Disaster #1, the project was still on schedule.

What *is* a problem?

When something goes wrong, we're dealing with cause and effect and, therefore, with Purposes, Things, and their Characteristics. A problem is simply an effect that's at odds with, contradicts, or frustrates your Purpose and it can be explained, solved, and overcome by focusing on the relevant Things and their Characteristics.

There are three basic types of problems:

1. You don't have the Things you need to achieve your Purpose

2. Some Things have the wrong Characteristics to achieve your Purpose

3. Some Things are obstacles keeping you from achieving your Purpose

Kate not having the manuals she needed was an example of missing things, Arnold making the head too big in his drawing was a Thing with a wrong Characteristic, and Ernie trying to sabotage the project was an obstacle.

What's *your* problem?

Before you can deal with a problem, you first have to correctly identify what the problem is, but it's very common to be wrong about what's wrong. Arnold, at first, thought he lacked artistic talent when what actually bothered him was that he didn't like his first attempt to draw the model. Nathan thought that there was an error in the computer code he wrote when the real problem was the line of code he *didn't* write – the one zeroing out the total before adding up the products.

To make sure you start off in the right direction, state the problem in terms of Things and their Characteristics. In our examples:

The Thing	The Characteristic
Arnold's drawing	Didn't look right to Arnold
Tutorial manuals	Kate didn't have them
Total on Nathan's report	Didn't add up correctly
Ernie	Was interfering with the project

Missing Things

If the problem is that you lack something you need, you can solve it by getting the missing Things – but that's not always easy or possible. Kate considered re-ordering her manuals but, at best, that would delay the project for three or four more days. At worst, the new order might suffer the fate of her last one.

At that point she had two options:

1. Doing without the Thing she wanted

2. Substituting another Thing that had the necessary Characteristics.

Teaching without the manuals was not a good idea. She knew the programmers wouldn't understand and remember the concepts if they were just abstract and theoretical. They needed real examples so that they could connect what she was saying with what they would actually be doing. In addition, she wanted each programmer to have something that they could jot their notes and questions on and use for later reference.

What other Thing could she substitute that had those Characteristics? After considering several possibilities, she decided on using an actual program she had written for another client. The program performed all the basic functions she wanted them to know – input and output, sorting, editing, updating, and reporting – and it was written in the programming style she wanted to use as the project standard. She printed out six copies, one for each programmer, and class was in session.

The wrong Characteristics

If you focus on the Characteristics of the Things that are a problem, it helps you find where the Things went wrong and guides you to fixing them by changing those Characteristics.

But Things with the wrong Characteristics are often the hardest type of problems to solve for two reasons. First, if something has the wrong Characteristic, you usually have to dig further to find out why and how it got that Characteristic. Second, if the Thing with the wrong Characteristic is a **person**, there is a great tendency to **blame**, which, even if justified, does little to actually solve the problem.

When Arnold stated his problem as "I can't draw," he was blaming himself. It wasn't just that he lacked drawing skills – something he could, in fact, acquire if he wanted to. It was that he was assuming that *he* was wrong for not drawing well and that it was a Characteristic he couldn't change.

Fortunately, his teacher guided him to focus on the relevant Things and Characteristics in greater detail. There was something Arnold didn't like about his *drawing*. What was it? It didn't look right. Why? He made the head too big. That was something he could – and did – fix.

Nathan was afraid he'd get blamed when he couldn't find the bug in his program and Kate sensed defensiveness in his insistence that every line of code he had written was correct. But Kate wasn't interested in blaming. Her focus was on finding the bug and fixing it. Since they didn't know where the total went wrong (acquired the wrong Characteristic), she suggested Nathan display the changing values of the total as the program ran.

Kate's approach to the "Ernie problem" wasn't to blame anyone either. What Ernie was doing was wrong and hurting the project so she had to deal with it, but first she had to find out *why* he was doing it and whether it was a Characteristic she could change. After she confronted him, it was clear that his Purpose and hers were and odds and there was nothing she could do to change it. Ernie was an obstacle.

Obstacles

When faced with an obstacle, you have two options:

    1. Remove the obstacle

    2. Avoid or work around the obstacle

Removing an obstacle is the obvious thing to do, but that might not be possible. The Vice President of the shipbuilding company would have loved to fire Ernie and replace him with someone who could do the job, but he couldn't because Ernie had political connections.

Since getting rid of Ernie wasn't an option, he resorted to workarounds. His first was to hire Kate to do the project and the second was to ignore the organization chart and have Kate report directly to him, taking Ernie out of the loop.

Dealing with problems step by step

When things go wrong, what should you do?

1. Have the right attitude toward the problem.

The best-laid plans go awry. It's always something. Stuff happens. Just keep problems in perspective.

Don't conclude that your troubles are due to some cosmic injustice and that the universe is conspiring against you. In fact, the world is really a friendly place where you can usually get what you want – but maybe not easily or right away.

Don't see the problem as a personal failure and proof of your unworthiness. All it really proves is that you don't know everything and sometimes you make bad choices. Welcome to the human race.

Instead, accept the fact that problems are **normal**. They happen as you go about pursuing and achieving your goals. Allow time and resources for them as Kate did using her "Two Major Disasters Rule."

Regard your problem as something you can deal with. If you're determined to find out why you got it wrong and what you can do to make it better, you'll **learn** from your errors. Mistakes teach you so much more than successes.

2. Identify what the problem is.

Begin by stating, in a single sentence, the Things and their Characteristics that are the problem. "The manuals are missing," "The total is wrong," etc. Your problem statement may turn out to be incorrect or lead to the discovery of a deeper underlying problem, but this is your starting point.

3. Classify the problem.

Determine if it's a missing Thing (go to Step 4), a Thing with the wrong Characteristics (go to Step 5) or an obstacle (go to step 6).

4. Missing Things

See if you can acquire the Things you're missing. If you can, get them and your problem is solved. If you can't get them, can you get along without them?

If not, try "Thing substitution." Look for another Thing that has the Characteristics you need. For instance, if you don't have paper clips to hold your papers together, how about using staples?

5. The wrong Characteristics

If you know that a Characteristic is wrong, can you change it? If the room is too cold, can you turn up the heat? If you don't know how to dance, can you take dancing lessons?

But in those cases where you don't know why a Thing acquired the wrong Characteristic, it can be very hard to fix it, so you need to find the cause. Why won't the lamp turn on? Is the bulb burned out? Is the lamp plugged in? Is the fuse blown? If you can't find the cause right away, try to localize the problem as to where and when it happened. If the radio plugged into the same outlet is working, it's not the fuse.

Watch out for the tendency to blame yourself or others. Accept the fact that you make mistakes – sometimes big mistakes – and maybe you could have or should have known better. So what? Even if the problem is your fault, beating yourself up about it does nothing to fix it. What's worse, it may lead you to act defensively and deny, avoid, or evade the problem. Not good. Instead, try to focus on what Characteristics are wrong with the Thing and what you can do to change those Characteristics.

If the problem involves the Characteristics of another person, your options for changing them are limited. For example, if you work with someone whose shrill, loud voice is driving you to distraction, you might let them know, privately and tactfully, how you feel and maybe they'll change. But maybe they won't. That's up to them, not you. If they can't or won't change, blaming won't help either. All you can do it treat them as an obstacle and go on to Step 6.

6. Obstacles

If you can, remove the obstacle. If you can't back your car out because you left the trash can in the driveway, move it out of the way.

If you can't get rid of the obstacle, try to avoid or work around it. If there's an accident on the way to work, take a different route. If you find your next-door neighbor unbearable, see if you can avoid him.

When you have a problem that's keeping you from getting what you want, look for the Things and Characteristics that caused it. That will guide you to understanding and correcting the problem.

It will also help you learn from your mistakes. While having problems isn't a good thing, if you pay attention to causes, you can learn a lot from your errors. That knowledge you gain will be filed in your Database of knowledge in the most efficient and accessible way – by Things and their Characteristics. Then it will be there when you need it and will help you avoid similar problems in the future.

CHAPTER 10

The WHYS of creativity

What is creativity? Is it an inborn talent? A mystical revelation? A rare ability? Not really.

Creating just means making something **new** that never existed before. It might be a work of art such as a story or a painting or an invention or scientific hypothesis or theory. It could also be the answer to a problem that appears suddenly in a flash of insight.

What does it take?

Creativity requires you to possess certain innate abilities, but that's not a problem. All you need are the basic human mental capacities you were born with. So what are those inner resources and how can you make the most of them?

A tale of two writers

Stanley's best-selling mystery books were popular and other writers admired their literary qualities and ingenious plots. Yet each one was written in about a month and some in as little as two weeks. How did he do it?

Stanley began by writing the end of each book first. In those final paragraphs, his hard-boiled detective hero revealed the murderer and how he had figured out whodunit. Once Stanley knew how he wanted his book to end, he let his imagination loose creating the characters, events, evidence, red herrings, and plot twists leading up to it.

Writing also came easily to Marilyn, the author of a dozen young adult novels now delighting a second generation of readers, but until she finished writing a book, she had no idea what would happen in her story or how it would turn out. "I know the characters and their basic situation," she said, "but that's all. The rest just flows out of my fingers and onto the page."

How could Stanley and Marilyn write so well and so effortlessly? Although their approaches might seem quite different, what common things were both of them doing that helped them to create? How can you do it too?

Capturing the light

Jose was caught by the sight of the park on that late winter afternoon.

The trees were bare, but some had buds about to become leaves and blossoms. Between patches of snow, the grass was showing hints of green. A little boy ran down the hill, his heavy jacket wide open and flapping in the breeze as his mother watched from below. But most of all Jose was intrigued by the light – cold and blue, clear and not quite bright, but with the promise of brightness and warmth. That, above all, said "Spring is coming," and he wanted to capture that light, that moment, and that feeling forever. He decided to paint it.

He thought and sketched. He would paint the park scene, but simplified. Just one tree. The hill wasn't important so he put it in the distant background. He didn't plan to include the little boy but he liked something about him. What was it? His carelessly open jacket. Instead of the boy, he wanted two people. Lovers. No, two friends *about to become* lovers. How could he show that? They could be walking together a normal distance apart for friends, but not close enough for lovers. OK. But how could he relate the two figures in a way that suggested romance? Eye contact. Instead of looking ahead, they would suddenly turn to look at each other. He would show the motion of that moment in the folds and creases of their clothing and especially in the woman's open coat as she turned to face the man.

He drew the scene he would soon paint as "The Promise of Spring": a vast, clear, cold blue sky dominating, the ground with patches of snow and beginning-to-green grass, and the two figures on the path with the tree branches above them silhouetted against the cold blue sky.

Once he had his final sketch, the actual painting was the easy part. Years and years of study and practice had taught him how to mix colors and apply them to the canvas to get exactly the effect he wanted. He set to work purposefully and joyfully.

Eureka!

Archimedes, the brilliant ancient Greek mathematician, had a problem. The king had given a jeweler a bar of gold and asked him to make it into a crown in the shape of a laurel wreath. Although the crown weighed the same as the original bar of gold, the king suspected that the jeweler had substituted a cheaper metal for part of the gold, but he couldn't prove it. That's when he called in Archimedes and gave him the job of finding out if the crown really was solid gold.

How could Archimedes tell? He couldn't take the crown apart or melt it down. As he thought about it, he walked to the public baths as he did every day. Still thinking about the crown, he stepped into a tub of water. As he lowered himself into the tub, the water began to spill out over the sides. Archimedes was curious and continued to lower himself slowly into the water. He noticed that the more his body sank into the water, the more water ran out over the sides of the tub.

He had the solution to the king's problem! He jumped out of the tub and ran, stark naked, through the streets shouting *"Eureka, Eureka!"* – which in Greek means, 'I found it! I found it!'

Archimedes had found a method for measuring the volume of an irregularly-shaped object.

What did Archimedes do to set himself up for that flash of insight and how can *you* do it when you have a tough problem to solve?

Where do creative ideas come from?

Marilyn's book was about Ryan and his adventures as a freshman at Avondale High. Where did all the specific details of her story come from?

The kitchen in Ryan's house was like the kitchen in the house Marilyn lived in when she was eight and the living room looked like the one in her favorite TV situation comedy. Ryan himself was a combination of her late husband Sam, her son Josh, and Marilyn's brother Mike. Ryan's wacky and brilliant best buddy looked and behaved very much like Marilyn's nephew.

In one way or another, every element in her story came from her own observations and experiences. Although the elements were recombined and rearranged in new ways, they all came from the same place: her **Database** of stored knowledge and experience.

On the rare occasions when she didn't have the information she needed in her Database, she got stuck. For example, she drew a blank when she tried to write a scene about Ryan's first attempt to ask a girl out on a date. The words just wouldn't come. She realized it was because she had no idea what that was like from a *boy's* point of view. It was time to do some research.

She asked her brother Mike and her son Josh, now grown with a teen-aged son of his own, if they could recall what they felt, what they did, and what happened the first time they asked a girl out. Mike couldn't remember anything, but that was typical of her not very introspective brother. Fortunately, Josh, as sensitive and perceptive as his mom, spent over an hour describing the hopes, fears, and triumph of that occasion in great detail. That was all Marilyn needed. She sat down at her desk and wrote the scene in five minutes.

Your Data Miner and the Creative Flow

If creative ideas and insights come from your Database, how do you get them out of there when you need them? How do you unleash a Creative Flow of ideas? The same way you remember things: by using your **Data Miner** as we discussed in Chapter 6.

To get your Creative Flow going, you first have to have a clear and emotionally arousing **Purpose**. Our two writers, the painter, and Archimedes certainly did. Stanley wanted to tell a story that set up and led to the ending he had written, Marilyn wanted to write about the adventures of an appealing fourteen-year-old boy in a way that would interest and inspire her young readers, Jose wanted to capture that cold, clear light in a scene that conveyed The Promise of Spring, and Archimedes wanted to prove whether or not the king's crown was solid gold.

It's also important to consciously note, as much as possible, the **Characteristics** of **Things** which you experience or remember. As we saw in Chapter 6, that's how you fill and organize your Database in a way that makes the information easiest to find.

Stanley, Marilyn, and Jose had always been aware and consciously identified the Characteristics relevant to their art during most of their experiences. Jose focused on the visual aspects of things – the light and shadows, colors, arrangement of objects, etc. As Stanley was having a beer in Duffy's Bar, he'd amuse himself by describing in words, as if he were writing it in a story, the place, the other people around him, etc.

Likewise, Marilyn paid attention to the Things and Characteristics that aroused her interest and she consciously identified what they were. As a child, she noted what gave her mother's kitchen such a comforting, homey feeling: the white wooden kitchen table where she dropped her books before she went to the fridge for an after-school snack, the pineapple-shaped cookie jar, the smell of bacon on Sunday mornings, etc.

As a result, the words and ideas were right there when the writers needed them. For instance, Stanley once took a shortcut through an alley that was so narrow that he thought, "If I was fatter, I'd have to go all the way around the block." That's how "alley" (Thing), "narrow" (Characteristic), and "fat man can't go through" (Characteristic) got stored in Stanley's Database. Years later, when his hero was being chased by a Mafia hit man who looked like the fat bartender at Duffy's, the idea of the detective escaping by going into an extremely narrow alleyway popped into Stanley's head.

Data connections

As we saw in Chapter 6, everything you've ever experienced is stored somewhere in your Database. Things you saw, heard, felt, etc. at the same time – the entire undifferentiated experience – are stored together because your mind automatically **associates** things that happen at the same time.

Association is the automatic default but not necessarily the best way to store information, particularly if you want to connect what you know in new and creative ways. Creativity is much more than just associative memory.

That's another reason why having your knowledge organized by Characteristics is so useful. It's not only effective for recalling specific information from your Database, but it's especially important when you're being creative because you're not merely remembering and duplicating what you already know. You're making something that never existed before out of **pieces** of your knowledge which you're rearranging and recombining in **new** ways.

Those pieces are the *selected* Characteristics of the Things you know. In real life, Stanley's alley was a shortcut that went from street to street, but in his story he made it a dead end and he had his detective escape by slipping through a bedroom window that faced the alley. (And that's how his hero met the beautiful Miss DeVane.)

The kitchen in Marilyn's book had the same homey Characteristics of the one she remembered from childhood, but in her story, when Ryan came home from school and got a snack, he put the cold pizza into a microwave which Marilyn's mother never had.

"Chance favors the prepared mind." – Louis Pasteur

If you have a clear, precise, and motivating Purpose and have stored your knowledge by Characteristics, you've done just about all of the required Prep Work. The Creative Flow will begin as your Data Miner provides you with much more than a combination by association. It will give you entirely new Things combined and integrated by essential Characteristics in accordance with your Purpose. If you're writing fiction, it will automatically feed you plots, characters, descriptions, and words. If you're a painter, it will provide you with visual arrangements, colors, and painting techniques. If you're a scientist, it will give you insights and hypotheses.

Is that all it takes? Mostly. You may need to define your Purpose more precisely, as Jose did when he sketched out the scene before he painted it, or as Stanley usually did by making a rough chapter outline of his book's plot.

You can also prepare a physical environment that's conducive to your Creative Flow, but that's a very personal thing. Stanley went fishing, taking along a six-pack of beer and a legal pad to write on. When he got home, he turned on a rock and roll music station, poured himself a beer, and typed up what he had scribbled while fishing. At 9 AM, Monday through Friday, Marilyn closed the door of her sound-proofed office, sat down at her desk and looked at the picture of "Ryan" – a smiling teenaged boy whose picture she had cut out of an ad. Then she put her fingers on the keyboard and told Ryan's story as if she were talking to Emma Zimmer, her target reader, a typical thirteen-year-old fan.

Getting stuck and unstuck

Ideally, with adequate Prep Work, all you need to do is relax, let the creative ideas flow freely, and simply capture and record them. But what if the ideas aren't flowing and you're stuck? It happens to creative people all the time, but it can be overcome if you understand what caused the problem.

The two most common reasons for creative blocks are that you don't have a sufficiently defined Purpose and/or the knowledge you need isn't in your Database.

Defining your purpose

Creating something new is just like achieving any goal and the same principles discussed in Chapter 8 apply here.

1. First, make your goal as specific and as detailed as needed to get your Creative Flow started.

All Marilyn needed to get going was wanting to tell about Ryan's first year of high school. She began by describing his hopes and expectations as he dressed for the first day at Avondale, described the other kids on the school bus (including Carly who would become his love interest), what the school looked like from the inside, etc. and she was on her way.

2. Then break the job down into tasks, as necessary. If the job is too big, separate it into smaller pieces.

Stanley found that merely writing his ending wasn't enough. Writing *everything* necessary to get there was too big an assignment, but he converted it into something manageable. Like Jose thinking about and sketching his final painting, Stanley began by imagining what kind of characters, events, and scenes he could include and making notes. He played with the possibilities for a while and then used his notes to construct a chapter by chapter outline in chronological order leading up to his final scene. Then he could write. While the goal of doing a whole book was daunting, writing a single chapter was easy.

Filling your Database

If your Purpose is clear, the ideas may still not flow because the information isn't in your Database. That's what happened when Marilyn got stuck trying to describe Ryan asking for a date and she resolved it by gathering the information she needed from her son.

Archimedes was stuck because he didn't know how to tell if the crown was solid gold but, unlike Marilyn, he couldn't ask someone because, in those days, *nobody* knew. But then Archimedes did something you can do too.

Remember the **Standing Orders** we discussed in Chapter 6 when Lou was trying to recall the name of "what's-his-name," the actor who starred in the movie with Doris Day?

> [A Standing Order is] a request for your Data Miner to be on
> the lookout for the missing information and that's how Lou
> eventually remembered "Rock Hudson." Lou set a Standing
> Order using "what's-his-name" as a placeholder for the
> information he was trying to recall.

When you set a Standing Order, your Data Miner will start looking for it
in your Database if it's in there or in your current and future experiences
if it's not. As you go about your daily activities, it will be on the lookout
for what you want, especially if you give your Data Miner a very specific
assignment as Archimedes did.

He asked his Data Miner to find him the answer to the question, "How
can I measure the volume of an irregularly-shaped object?" The answer
wasn't in his database, so Archimedes stopped thinking about it
consciously and went for a bath. But his Data Miner didn't stop. It kept
on looking for the answer and, when the Greek lowered himself into the
tub and the water ran over the sides, *Eureka!*

Reality Testing

Whatever your Data Miner pulls out of your Database or gathers from
current experiences may or may not be exactly what you're looking for.
Like the messages contained in emotional reactions, it has to be evaluated
and Reality Tested. Your Creative Flow may give you some good ideas
and a lot of junk. You have to be brutally honest with yourself as you
evaluate what comes out of your Database. Some material will not suit
your Purpose at all and you'll have to throw it out and try again. Others
will have some merit, but need to be refined, clarified, and edited.

After Archimedes had his *"Eureka!"* moment, he checked it out to see
if he was right. He took an amount of gold equal to the weight of the
crown and an amount of silver of the same weight. Then he filled a large
vessel to the brim with water, dropped the silver into it, and measured
how much water ran out. Then he did the same with the gold. He found
that less water ran out with the gold, because the gold was denser than
the silver.

Finally, he filled the vessel again and dropped the king's crown into the
water and found that more water ran out than for an amount of gold of
the same weight. That proved that the crown wasn't solid gold.

Writers need to Reality Test too. Both Stanley and Marilyn effortlessly produced their first drafts, but after that got down to the serious and often difficult and frustrating work of editing.

When Stanley began his writing career, he had a tendency to over-write, say too much, repeat himself, and include unnecessary details. He would read his work over and over looking for those flaws and rewriting to eliminate and correct them. By the time he was done, his edited text was a third the size of his first draft and much more powerful.

That's how he became such a good writer. In the process of editing his work, he learned a lot about the best ways of expressing, describing, and communicating what he had to say. That knowledge was all there in his Database when he wrote his later books and his first drafts became shorter and tighter and needed much less editing. The editing he did on his first book became the most important Prep Work for his subsequent books.

Creativity step by step

You possess powerful mental abilities you can use to develop new insights and ideas and produce inventions, solutions, and works of art. Here's how to do it.

1. Have a clear and specific Purpose.

If you can, state what you want to do in a single sentence such as "I want to capture the light and the feeling of coming Spring," or "I want to solve the problem of ..." If you can't get specific enough to one-sentence it, play with the possibilities, consider alternatives, and move in the direction of what most appeals to you. Eventually a clear and specific goal will begin to emerge.

2. Identify the Things and Characteristics you're working with.

What are you dealing with? A beer-drinking detective with a passion for justice? An endearing teen-age boy facing the challenges of a new school? A park scene with a cold, clear, blue sky? An irregularly-shaped object which may or may not be solid gold? Or?

3. Do additional Prep Work as needed.

If you've done Steps 1 and 2 and the Creative Flow hasn't started, what's the problem? Is the job too big? Then break it down into smaller tasks, outline or sketch your final goal, and see if you can start to work on a *part* of the job.

Do you need to gather more information? What, specifically do you need to know?

Are you being annoyed or distracted by what's going on around you? Then pick a time and place where you can work without such disturbances. Is there anything that helps you relax and get in the mood for creative work? Playing music? Taking a bath? Having a beer?

4. Relax and let it flow.

Capture and record what's coming out of your Database and *that's all*. Don't censor, evaluate, edit, or critique. What you're getting doesn't have to be perfect or even good. Just let it flow. You'll have plenty of time to fix it in the next step, but right now just get it all out.

If the Creative Flow stops before you've reached your goal, identify what the problem is and go back to Step 1, 2, or 3 to do whatever additional Prep Work you need to do to get unstuck.

5. Reality Test.

Once you've got something, evaluate it. Is it *exactly* what you wanted? Probably not. Can you fix it or should you discard it and try again? If you want to use it but it needs fixing and you're not sure how to do it, try the problem solving techniques in Chapter 9.

If you're already a creative person, understanding the WHYS of the process will make you even more so. If a creative activity is something new for you, try the techniques and suggestions in this chapter and you might discover talents and abilities you didn't know you had.

CHAPTER 11

Teachers, experts, and advisors

How much of your knowledge did you discover all by yourself and how much did you learn from your parents, teachers, and friends, or from things you read? Most of what you know came from other people, didn't it? Yet sometimes what others tell you is wrong and if you accept what they say uncritically, you'll be wrong too. Fortunately, there's a *WHYS Way* to validate what you learn from others.

When you need to do something and you don't have the time or the interest to get the necessary knowledge, it makes sense to hire an expert like a doctor, lawyer, accountant, architect, etc. But can you rely on what they tell you? Do they really know what they're talking about? There's a *WHYS Way* to make the most of experts without becoming an expert yourself.

Then there are all the people who are constantly giving you advice about what you should do – what you should eat, how you should spend your money or your time, etc. Can you trust advisors, consultants, advertisers, politicians, and peers pressuring you to do something? Is what they're telling you to do in your best interests? There's a *WHYS Way* to figure that out.

Most adults usually have beneficial relationships with those they consult and learn from – but not always. Even people who are very good judges of others are occasionally led astray or taken advantage of by someone they trusted and relied on. How can you avoid this happening to you?

Let's look at three simple and, perhaps, obvious, examples that show how, by finding and validating **causes**, you can have more consistently good outcomes when you deal with teachers, experts, and advisors.

The formula

"Why did you use that formula to calculate the stresses on the suspension bridge?" Leroy asked his engineering professor.

"Everybody uses the formula. It works," he replied.

"But WHY does it work?" Leroy insisted.

"Darned if I know," replied the professor.

Leroy was unhappy with that answer so he did further research. He looked up the formula and found out how it was derived. It made sense, but he also discovered that there were other ways to calculate the stresses. Although his professor's formula was commonly used, it wasn't the best one to use for a suspension bridge. It grossly over-estimated the amount of steel needed for the supports. Sure, the bridge wouldn't fall down, but it would be so much more expensive to build.

Was the professor a good teacher? Why or why not?

Back trouble

Dr. Kramer was the most famous back doctor in New York. He was also the most expensive, but at this point, Darlene didn't care. She had been in agony since her back went out a month ago and nothing she had tried on her own had worked.

When she finally saw Dr. Kramer, he didn't seem to have read any of the medical information forms she filled out or know her case and he didn't ask any questions. He just bragged about his Harvard education, being the president of an important professional association, and treating some famous, but unnamed, celebrities. Then he dashed off a prescription for a pain-killer saying "This should work and, if it doesn't, we can always do surgery," and sent her on her way.

Before Darlene filled the prescription, she looked up the drug and found that it was very powerful – and very addictive. She was also afraid of surgery because her father's back surgery had made his condition worse. She wanted a second opinion.

She made an appointment to see Dr. Greta Leaf, the author of *Bye-Bye Bad Backs*. Darlene noted that the forms she filled out at Dr. Leaf's office had more questions about her current complaint, when it started, how she had tried to treat it, etc. There was also a place to describe her father's slipped disc.

"I've been reading over your medical history and I have some questions," Dr. Leaf said. After she asked them, she had Darlene stand up, try to touch her toes, and make a dozen other moves noting her range of motion and which ones were most painful. Then Dr. Leaf sent her to get x-rays.

"Your back looks fine," she said, pointing to the x-rays, "but the way you stand and walk strains your back muscles. When you told me it hurt, those muscles were in spasm. Normally, your back and tummy muscles – your abdominals – share the load, but you sit at a desk all day. Your abdominals can get weak. I'd like you to strengthen them and also to improve your flexibility and posture by doing the exercises in Chapter 9 twice a day," she said, handing her a copy of her book. "Let's see if it helps. Any questions?"

Darlene asked about the exercises and what she could do to deal with her pain and Dr. Leaf answered everything to her satisfaction. Then the doctor told her to make a follow-up appointment in two weeks and call her any time she had a problem or a question.

If you had back trouble, which doctor would you go to: Dr. Kramer or Doctor Leaf? Why? What did the doctors do differently and why is the difference important?

Advice from family and friends

"What are you waiting for? Your biological clock to run out?" Rachel's mother asked in a voice calculated to make her feel guilty. "You want Geordie to be an only child like you were? Believe me, if I hadn't messed up my insides giving birth to you, I would have had more children. Now you're my last chance for another grandchild." Rachel didn't know what to say.

She was still quite upset when she had lunch with her best girlfriend Jane, the mother of three rambunctious boys.

"I've been considering having another baby," said Rachel, "but I'm not sure I'd be doing the right thing. What should I do? You have three. What do you think?"

"My three guys are perfect for me," said Jane, "but you're not me. Think about what you could gain and lose from having another one and how it would affect your life and your marriage. "

"Well, Geordie's six and in school all day, so he needs less of my time and attention. David has been a terrific father to Geordie and when we talked about another baby he said 'Anything you want is fine with me.' I was looking forward to going back to work full-time. We could just about afford another one if I worked, but that means the baby would have to be in daycare and I don't like that. A child should have a full-time parent for the first five or six years."

"Those are all good reasons to not have another baby, Jane observed. "What are your reasons *for* doing it."

"Well, it would get my mother off my back!"

Jane smiled, and said, "So the *real* problem isn't about having a baby; It's about your mother. Does having a baby for *her* make sense?"

"Of course not, but what do I do when she brings the subject up?"

"Don't argue and don't agree," Jane advised. "You're a loser either way. Just listen politely and sympathetically. Say something like 'That would be very nice,' or 'You're a terrific Grandma,' or 'David and I are thinking it over.' Be pleasant and truthful, but non-committal. You get the idea."

"That makes sense, Jane."

Who gave Rachel better advice – her mother or Jane? Why?

What do you want to know?

Experts are people who have special skills or knowledge in some particular field and you use them when they know something you don't know, but need to know. Darlene needed to know how to stop the pain in her back, Leroy was studying to be a structural engineer, and Rachel didn't really solicit her mother's advice, but once she got it, she sought Jane's help in dealing with it.

The first thing is to find somebody who knows what *you* need to know because, while a particular person can provide the knowledge that satisfies the Purposes of many people, it may not be sufficient for you. Leroy's professor was a good teacher for most of the students in the class who were architecture majors getting a sense of the structural issues of building, but not for Leroy. He wanted to build bridges and needed more in depth knowledge.

Who's an expert?

Do the people you consult actually have the knowledge you need? The world is full of people making dubious claims about knowing the secret of losing twenty pounds in ten days or making millions in real estate. If they all really knew what they were talking about, there would be a lot more skinny millionaires out there.

So how can you tell a real expert from a phony?

Did the doctor graduate from a prestigious medical school or a diploma mill? Check out credentials. Does the roofer have a long list of satisfied customers? Ask for references and check out reviews. Was the interior decorator recommended by your friend with the drop-dead gorgeous living room? Has the investment advisor's portfolio done better than the stock market for the past twenty years? Assess what you do know or can find out.

Checking credentials, references, recommendations, and work history won't tell you for sure whether someone really knows his stuff – it may lead you to Dr. Kramer before Dr. Leaf – but it's a good place to start. It will give you at least *some* evidence about who they are and some **reasons** for relying on – or distrusting – them.

Do they explain WHY?

Since you don't yet know what the teacher, expert, or advisor knows, can you trust what they say or what they want you to do? Their advice could be colored by their own prejudices or personal Purposes which may be at odds with yours. Asking them **why** can help you distinguish the facts you need from opinions you shouldn't rely on.

Until you find the **cause** that explains **why** Things are what they are or do what they do, you can't know anything with absolute certainty. Until you can find the cause, you should use the knowledge you do have – or can obtain – to get closer and closer to the cause and to certainty. From the section on "Seeking certainty" in Chapter 5 of this book:

> As for the unknowns, even if you don't know the cause with absolute certainty, when you use the correct method, you'll be getting closer and closer to it. You may not learn everything you want to know, but with each step on the road to truth you'll understand more and more and be able to act with greater effectiveness and self-confidence.

Use the same methods when you're getting your information from other people as when you're investigating the world on your own. **Seek causes.**

Does your teacher tell you **why** what he says is true? Does your accountant tell you **why** you're not eligible for the tax deduction? Does your broker tell you **why** he recommends Stock A over Stock B? If you ask, can they explain **why** in terms you can understand?

If they can't, be suspicious. It may mean they don't have the information you want.

Does what they tell you make sense?

There's no reason to question or doubt everything someone else tells you, but you shouldn't take them on faith either. You may not know as much as *some* people do, but you do know what you do know. If anything a teacher, expert, or advisor says contradicts something you know for a fact, watch out! Contradictions always mean that someone and/or something is **wrong**.

Does the "miracle wrinkle serum" just make your wrinkles shinier, your skin stickier, and your wallet lighter? Does your math teacher ignore the textbook and spend class time on political rants that contradict everything you know about history and human nature? Does your broker recommend a stock his company is underwriting that seems too risky? He may have a Purpose (earning a big commission) that's at odds with yours (financial security).

Whatever you do, **never ignore contradictions**. Don't assume that when someone contradicts what you know, that they are right and you are wrong, but don't assume that you're right and they're wrong either. **Reality Test it**.

Also, pay attention to your gut feelings of distrust and uneasiness when dealing with authorities and experts. Those are "alarm system" emotions telling you that something is wrong. Even if you can't immediately identify exactly where the contradictions are, don't ignore your doubts. They may have a perfectly valid cause. Keep looking using the introspection techniques in Chapter 7.

Dealing with teachers, experts, and advisors step by step

1. Be clear about what you want to know.

What do you want to know that requires outside expertise? Do a little preliminary research on the subject. Sometimes this may be sufficient.

If it isn't, it will often guide you to what kind of people can best help you and what questions you should ask them.

2. Have evidence that the teacher, expert, or advisor has the knowledge you want.

Check credentials and get references and referrals. Read something they've written. See if you can sit in on a class or have a preliminary consultation. Then evaluate what you've seen. Do they seem knowledgeable and does what they say make sense? Does anything they say or do give you pause or concern?

3. Get a causal explanation in terms you can understand.

Expect them to tell you **why** they do, say, or recommend the things they do. If you still need to know more before you can trust their opinions and conclusions, **ask**.

4. Reality Test what they tell you.

You should check out and test the knowledge and opinions of other people in exactly the same way you check out your own ideas, hunches, and hypotheses. If you can take what someone else tells you and use it to find causal connections that pass the Certainty Test, you can be as sure and as certain as if you thought them up all by yourself.

Other people have so much to offer you. When you know how to make the most of the knowledge and insights of the right teachers, experts, and advisors, it will expand and enhance your life enormously.

CHAPTER 12

The WHYS teacher

What's the best way to teach what you know to other people? How do you show a friend the right way to use your power tools? If you're a parent, what's the best way to help your children with their homework or teach them how to ride a bike? If you're a teacher, how can you present your subject so that your students will understand – and most of all – *retain* the material?

Let's see how LuAnn and Phil did it.

Grandma's computer

When LuAnn asked Grandma how she liked the video of her great-grandchild Gina's first steps, she got a blank stare. It seems the only thing Grandma ever did with the computer they gave her last Christmas was leaving it sitting on her desk and dusting it occasionally.

"I'm too old to learn complicated machines," said Grandma. "Your father tried. Motherboards! Interfaces! I know what mothers and faces are, but the rest of that is beyond me."

LuAnn, recalling how her father had tried teaching her to drive a car by giving her a lecture on internal combustion engines, immediately saw what the problem was. "It's not complicated, Grandma. It's as easy as shopping for groceries and you do that just fine. Like to see Gina? I'll show you how."

LuAnn sat Grandma down in front of the computer, had her turn it on, and showed her how to point with the mouse. "See this heart on the screen that says 'Hughstone Family?' Point to the heart and press this button on the mouse – click. That's it. What do you see?"

"There's you and your dad and mom and your sisters! Where's Gina?"

"See if you can guess. Point to something you think might be it and click on it," and Grandma did.

"I did it wrong. That's just your sister Patty."

"You're doing fine. When you go to a store and don't find what you want right away, you keep on looking, right?" LuAnn said as she showed

Grandma how to go back and try again. Then Grandma clicked on "Videos" and seeing "Gina walks!," clicked on that. As the video played, Grandma was amazed, enthralled, and very proud of herself.

"How do I play it again?" she asked and LuAnn showed her.

"I have to go now," LuAnn said, "but there's a lot you'll like on our family website. Just click on different things and see what happens. Want to know the latest family news? Next time I'll show you how to do email."

What did LuAnn do to get Grandma interested in the computer? How did she make learning easy for Grandma? What did LuAnn do right that her father did wrong?

The new math teacher

"Pennick is quitting to take a job in aerospace," the principal of Leesdale High announced, "so next year you'll be teaching his algebra classes."

"But I'm a music teacher!" Phil gasped. "I got certified in math twenty years ago, but I never taught it."

"The kids adore you and hang on your every word and you'll have the whole summer to get ready. I'm sure you'll be fine."

Phil wasn't so sure, especially after he looked at the algebra text. No wonder the kids had given *Multicultural Mathematics* by Jenck and Krep the nickname "Junk and Crap." There were lots of pictures, random word problems, and complex equations presented six chapters before anything was said about what an equation basically *was*. Algebra was presented in such a disorganized and disconnected way that Phil's reaction was "How can anybody ever learn from *this* thing?"

He located a copy of his old high school algebra text in a used bookstore and it confirmed two things: first, that the math was useful and fascinating and, also, that there was a logical, reasonable way of presenting it. He used this old text and several other books to review and relearn algebra, as well as to gain more advanced knowledge of math than was required for his classes. Then he spent the rest of the summer making his own lesson plans based on the old, logical way he had been taught math. Each of his lessons would allow his students to thoroughly master one concept at a time by defining what the concept meant, showing where it came from, and how it was related to what the students already knew.

On the first day of class Phil faced his students with his usual bouncing self-confidence and humor because he now had a solid grasp of algebra and was eager to share it. He showed them why math was cool and his enthusiasm was catching.

Phil's biggest challenge was teaching individuals who varied from Cindy who had already flunked algebra twice to Hank who had been homeschooled, had mastered algebra when he was nine, and was just taking the class to get credit for it.

He gave Cindy special attention to make sure she got each concept and could keep up with the class. Within a month, she was doing fine on her own. "You're so much better than Mr. Pennick and his stupid algebra book. You make it easy," she said.

He offered Hank challenging advanced work, which he took to eagerly, and told him he could skip class if he wanted to.

"And miss your crazy jokes? No way!"

What did Phil have to learn to teach the algebra classes? Why did he make his own lesson plans instead of using the school's textbook? What made his teaching so effective?

Why people learn

As we saw way back in Chapter 1, we are always asking "Why?" because throughout life we need knowledge in order to make good choices and to take the right actions to get what we want. We constantly need to know the WHYS – the causes and reasons for things – in order to achieve our Purposes. That's the motivation to learn. But if someone doesn't see the value, to them, of what you want to teach them, why should they bother learning it?

That's why, when you're teaching, your first order of business is motivating your students and making sure their Purpose is wanting to know what you have to teach them.

Motivational Tips

One way to engage people is to ask a question they don't know the answer to but you will eventually provide. "What are the rings of Saturn made of?" "How did a poor boy like Benjamin Franklin become one of the richest men in Colonial America?" "What's an easy trick for multiplying by 5?" This makes them want to know the WHYS that answer your questions.

Another way is to promise information if they stick around and pay attention. Right before the commercial break, the anchor on the TV newscast said, "Coming up: How you can prepare for the horrible weather tomorrow. Why the Mayor called the Police Chief a liar. The basketball superstar who granted a gravely ill child's wish." Those promises of information were calculated to keep viewers from changing the channel. Similarly, LuAnn motivated Grandma to use the computer with the promise of seeing the video of Gina.

Most important is showing the potential *personal* value, to the student, of knowing what you're about to teach. An excellent example of doing this is the way Dr. Leonard Peikoff, in his lectures on "Teaching Johnny to Think," [12] suggested introducing the study of literature to eight- to ten-year-olds. He told them

> You are growing up and deciding what kind of person you are going to be. Wouldn't it be useful to have an indication of all the different types of human beings, like a menu at a restaurant? This is really what literature is. It is like a menu of the kinds of human beings, what to expect from them and an exercise in seeing if one trait leads to another.[13]

Peikoff also stressed that the enthusiasm of the instructor and their commitment to the subject is vital. The teacher should communicate, "This is urgent. This is crucial. I love it; it is really exciting. ... Regard your teaching as acting and whip up a storm of excitement."[14] Phil certainly did, and that was one of his secrets for being such an effective and popular teacher.

While learning is usually an enjoyable experience, every subject has its difficult and arid stretches, so Peikoff endorsed anything reasonable that will make learning a pleasurable experience.

That is why I am a strong advocate of humor as a part of any presentation. ... If you can make them laugh, it helps give them the idea that this process is not quite so tedious. It also helps to keep them awake. [15]

Organizing the material

If you treat the goal of educating your students just like any other goal and apply the principles discussed in Chapter 8, you can effectively teach even the most complex and difficult subjects. Just as a big project should be broken down into small sub-tasks, you should break the job of teaching down into **lessons**, each with its own sub-goal, and then lay out the lessons in causal order.

Since we either get knowledge directly from our five senses or derive it from previous experiences and conclusions, causal order means that the lessons should be presented so that the students can perceive and/or relate the new material to what they already know. Ask yourself, "What does someone need to know before he can learn this?" A child needs to understand counting before addition and addition before he can grasp multiplication. Since what happens causes what happens later, it's usually a good idea to teach history in chronological order.

Begin by identifying the Things you're talking about. Define your terms. Give examples and point out the essential Characteristics. When Phil introduced equations, he began with examples like "1 + 1 = 2" and "2 + 2 = 4." Then he pointed out that the quantity to the left of the equal sign was always the same as the quantity to the right of the equal sign.

Once everyone understood why the equality of both sides is an essential Characteristic of an equation, Phil built on that to explain what algebraic variables were. Phil erased one of the numbers, substituted an "x ", and asked what the value of "x" would have to be for both sides of the equation to be equal. Once they got that, he went on give them examples showing how practical and useful it is to use "x" as a placeholder when you're calculating and you don't know all the quantities.

Making it stick

What's the use of teaching something if the student memorizes unrelated facts just to pass a test and can't recall anything a week later? That's a waste of time and effort for both the teacher and the student.

A teacher's goal should be to get the students to learn the subject in a way that's easy to remember whenever they need it. How can you do that? You'll find the answer back in Chapter 6 where we discussed Data Mining and how we store and retrieve information.

As we saw there, one's Purpose not only guides and empowers thinking, but it's also important for successful data storage and Data Mining. If someone really, really *wants* to know something and he's emotionally invested in it, he'll remember it better. As was said in Chapter 6, "[W]hen something is very important – if it's associated with strong feelings like desire, happiness, fear or loss – it makes a stronger imprint."

Easier Data Mining is also a reason to present the material in causal order stressing the essential Characteristics of Things. While you can use memory tricks like "book-marking" to remember individual disconnected facts for the short-term – like where you parked your car in a big parking lot – this doesn't work in the long-run. To remember and have your knowledge handy when you need it, it's best to deliberately identify the Characteristics of Things which suit your Purpose.

That's why Phil didn't have his students memorize key formulas. Instead, he showed them, step by step, where the formula came from and why it was what it was. That way, if students forgot the exact formulation, they could figure out what it should be all by themselves.

Measuring progress

You can teach, but is your student learning? That's something you have to know, particularly with a subject like math where later knowledge requires the understanding and use of more basic concepts. If the students aren't getting it, you need to re-teach the material before you move on. So, how can you measure how much they have learned?

In traditional classrooms, students are given quizzes, tests, and exams, but this may not be the best way. If you wait until the final exam to find out that nobody has a clue about what you've been talking about all semester, it's too late to do anything about it. Even with weekly quizzes, it's better to know on Monday rather than waiting until Friday.

So check on what your students know as you go along.

1. Pause after each major point or new concept and give them a chance to use and to question the new ideas you've presented. LuAnn checked to make sure Grandma could navigate the web page with the mouse.

2. Solicit feedback and comments. Phil asked the students to give examples of what "x" means in an equation.

3. See if they can apply the information to a new situation. LuAnn challenged Grandma to find Patty's wedding pictures.

4. Ask them to explain the important Things, Characteristics and causal relationships. Phil asked "Why, when you add a quantity to one side of an equation, should you add exactly the same quantity to the other side of the equation?"

Teaching others step by step

1. Know your subject.

You can't teach what you don't know, so learn as much as you can about the subject you intend to teach. Of course, your knowledge will always be limited, so be honest about it. If students raise questions you can't answer, it's OK to say "I don't know" and to look it up or direct them to where they might find an answer.

2. Motivate the students to learn.

Respect their need to have *personal* reasons for wanting to know the subject and give them some. Indicate the payoffs. Express enthusiasm. Arouse their curiosity by asking questions and promising to give them useful and interesting information.

3. Organize and present the material systematically.

Break the subject down into lessons which are causally related to each other. Begin each lesson with something they can directly see or already know and then show them something new and how it relates to what they know. That way, the students won't be just memorizing disconnected facts and taking it on faith that what you say is true. They will understand *why* it is true.

4. Check to see if they have learned each lesson.

Get feedback as you go along to see how well the students understand each new idea or concept. Ask and answer questions and see if they can use the knowledge in new situations.

If you do it *The WHYS Way,* teaching what you know to another person can be fun and rewarding for *both* of you.

CHAPTER 13

The WHYS Way to persuade

Using the techniques described in the last chapter, it should be easy to communicate with people who already agree with you or are open to your message, but what if they're not? Often you have to deal with family members, friends, prospective customers, or enemies who are uninterested or opposed to you. Then what?

How can you get them interested? What can you do to convince them that you're right? How can you overcome their objections and get them on your side? There's a *WHYS Way* to do it. Let's consider three examples.

The super sales gal, the hopeful teen, and the candidate

Rose had been the company's top-selling realtor for the past eight years. She was especially adept at finding exactly the right house for a prospective buyer and closing the deal. We'll see how she did it.

Alex was about to turn 16 and get his driver's license. He had been looking forward to driving his dad's car all by himself, picking up his girlfriend for a date, and driving over to his friends' houses – until last night. When he brought the subject up at dinner, his father pounded the table so hard the dishes rattled. "You drive my car?" he shouted. "Over my dead body!" Fortunately for Alex, that wasn't the end of the story.

Paul wanted to be the new mayor. The Candidates' Forum was his big chance to show the voters why they should choose him and not the incumbent.

Having a Purpose

Before you can convince someone else, you have to define **your** Purpose. Why do you want to persuade them? What do you want them to do and why?

Rose's Purpose was to earn commissions by selling houses, so she needed to get people to buy the particular houses she earned commissions on. Alex wanted to drive a car all by himself. Paul wanted to get elected.

Knowing the subject

As we saw with teaching, anyone out to convince others should know their subject and be prepared to sell their message and prove their case in terms of the appropriate Things and Characteristics. For Rose, that meant knowing as much as she could about the homes currently on the market because those were the Things she was selling. She visited every new listing and noted the home's relevant Characteristics – any features that a buyer might desire.

Alex knew he'd have a problem changing his father's mind and the problem's name was Ralph. When Alex's older brother began driving the family car, all went well until Ralph went out drinking with his buddies. Driving home that night, he ran into a utility pole, totaled the car, and knocked out the power for six blocks. Alex knew his father was going to bring up Ralph and, when he did, Alex intended to remind him that he wasn't at all like his brother when it came to driving. He was a different Thing and he had significantly different Characteristics.

Paul knew why he would be a good mayor. His background as a CPA would help him straighten out the city's troubled finances, his views on public safety had won him the support of the town's policemen, and he had just been endorsed by the state's popular Governor. Those were Characteristics the voters wanted. His opponent, on the other hand, the corrupt and financially irresponsible current mayor, had presided over four years of increased crime, taxes and unemployment. Those were Characteristics the voters didn't want.

Asking and listening

Neither Rose, Alex, nor Paul began by presenting their own arguments. Instead, they asked and listened.

Rose

Before she showed a single home, Rose always sized up prospective buyers. She asked them many questions about what kind of house they could afford and the features and neighborhood they were interested in so she'd have an idea of what they wanted and why they wanted it.

Mr. and Mrs. Doyle asked to see homes in Jefferson Heights but, given how much they could put down and their income, that was out of the question. But Rose did have some properties in their price range and Jim Doyle was a carpenter, so she was ready when the Doyles came to see her.

"I hope someday I can sell you a home in Jefferson Heights," said Rose, "but that's the most expensive neighborhood in town. Even a vacant lot there costs much more than you said you could spend.

"Not to worry. I have three affordable homes close by. One's even in the J. H. school district. They're all run down and need a lot of work, but you're handy, Jim. If you fix one of them up, you can save a ton of money and sell it for a big profit in a few years. Would you like to see them?"

"Absolutely not," said Jim Doyle. "It's gotta be Jefferson Heights."

"Why?" asked Rose.

"That's what we came to see," he insisted, "that's why."

"It's out of your price range."

"So what? I don't care."

Alex

The next night before dinner, Alex said to his dad, "You were very upset when I mentioned driving your car. Tell me why." His father then launched into a long rant about how much Ralph had cost him, how irresponsible teenagers were, and how he had no intention of letting anyone drive his prized sports car – not even Alex's mother.

"Do you think I'm irresponsible like Ralph?" he asked and his father acknowledged that Alex was sensible, prudent, and could always be counted on to do the right thing.

"I know how much your car means to you, Dad. Would it be OK if Mom let me drive her car instead?" His father still objected.

"Do you know how much it will cost me for your car insurance? An arm and a leg! I'm not made out of money."

"I know. What if I pay for my own insurance?" His father tilted his head to one side and thought about it.

Paul

Before Paul showed up for the forum, he hired a polling firm to find out what the voters wanted.

40% were concerned with crime and 55% were unemployed or knew someone who was, but very few voters knew about the city's sorry financial condition and what caused it. 65% of likely voters were planning to vote for the current Mayor because they thought he was a nice guy who was doing a good job. They were dead wrong, but that was something Paul had to show them.

At the forum, when it was Paul's turn to speak, he began by addressing the audience and asking for a show of hands.

"How many people know that the Mayor gets paid $200,000 more than the Governor?"

"That the Mayor's brother got a no-bid contract for adding one room to the Police Academy for twice what it cost to build the whole complex three years ago?"

"Who's worried about their jobs? Crime? Property taxes?"

The unpersuadables

Sometimes, there is nothing you can say or do that will make a difference. Some people may just be unpersuadable.

Jim Doyle was being unreasonable, thought Rose. They're probably "Looky-Loos" who just want to gawk at the homes of the rich and famous. Since they weren't serious buyers, she was wasting her time with them.

"I'm afraid I can't help you," she said, "but if you change your mind, here are brochures on the three fixer-uppers I mentioned." As the Doyles were leaving, she added "They're going to have a Jefferson Heights Home Tour next month to benefit the Boys and Girls Club. Only $10 to see six fantastic mansions. Check it out."

Dad had a short fuse and Alex knew better than to argue with him when he first exploded at dinner. Nothing would get through as long as Dad was angry, so Alex held his tongue and bided his time. By the next day, his father had calmed down considerably, but he still needed to vent. When he did, his anger was fully spent and some important issues finally came out.

There was no way Paul was going get the votes of the Mayor and his cronies, so he didn't try. He spoke only to the rest of the audience, especially those who had raised their hands or reacted to his preliminary questions.

Focusing on areas of ignorance and agreement

Rose, Alex, and Paul, using key information gathered from asking and listening, went on from there.

If the Doyles were really interested in buying a home they could afford, Rose was prepared to help them find one. She tried to explain why Jefferson Heights wasn't the right neighborhood for them right now, but there was still a way to get what they said they wanted.

Once Alex focused on it, his father agreed that Alex was responsible and likely to be a good driver. Alex also agreed with his dad's desires to keep his sports car to himself and not have to pay for his son's insurance. That was OK because what Alex wanted was to drive all by himself and his mom's car would do just as well. Building on those areas of agreement, the only thing left for Alex to show was how, with a good student discount and a part-time job at the movie theater, he could pay for his own insurance.

Paul homed in on areas of ignorance. Most of the voters had no idea that the friendly, charming mayor they trusted had conned them and looted the city treasury, so Paul told them. As he laid out the facts in detail, the audience listened in stunned silence. The Mayor was unprepared for the barrage of angry questions that followed and the forum made headlines in the local newspaper.

How to persuade step by step

What Rose, Alex, and Paul did to persuade is based on ideas you're already familiar with. Here is the process.

1. Have a clear Purpose.

Identify what you want the other person to do. Do you want them to buy your product or idea, change what they're doing, cooperate with you on something, or agree with you? Have your Purpose clearly in mind.

2. Know your own viewpoint and the reasons for it.

As we've seen with teaching, you have to know your own subject well. If you're after honest agreement, what you say has to be true and you have to be able to explain **why** it is true.

3. Ask and listen.

Changing another person's mind is no different from changing anything else. You need to know the relevant Things and Characteristics. The person you're trying to win over is the important Thing. He already has an opinion and reasons for it and those are his relevant Characteristics. You need to know what they are. That's why, before you try to make your own points, you should begin by asking questions and listening. Your goal is to find out three things: (1) the other person's Purpose, (2) his areas of agreement with you, and (3) the areas of ignorance or factual disagreement.

4. Find their Purpose.

As we discussed in the last chapter, when you're trying to teach somebody something, they won't pay attention or accept what you have to say unless they have a Purpose of their own for listening to you. When you start with people who aren't interested in your message or disagree with you, it's usually because they have a Purpose that's at odds with yours.

They may think you're not worth their time or that you're wrong, they may want to win the argument even if they know you're right, they may have a deeper concern than their stated objection, or they may have some other reason that even they may be unaware of. Since that's what's standing in your way, you must begin by finding out what their Purpose is, what they believe, and why. You do that by **asking** them.

In sales, this process is called "qualifying" a prospective buyer. By asking what he wants, you cannot only find out what kind of Thing he's in the market for, but the particular Characteristics he wants it to have. If the buyer isn't sure what he wants – which is often the case – you can help him define his Purpose and show him why what you have to offer will satisfy his needs.

That's why Rose inquired as to why the Doyles wanted to buy a house and then suggested the three fixer-uppers. That's also how Alex found out that his dad's real Purpose was to protect his sports car and save his money. Once Alex knew that, he could offer acceptable solutions.

5. Find areas of agreement.

Ask questions that could identify areas of agreement. If you find them and the other person agrees with you that a certain goal is desirable or something is true and important, that's the best foundation to build your argument on. It defines a common Purpose which can change the situation from "you vs. him" to the two of you working together to achieve the same thing.

For example, Paul appealed to most of the voters who agreed with him about having honest, cost-effective government rather than crime, unemployment, and corruption. Building on that, he explained why he could give them what they wanted much better than the current mayor.

6. Find areas of ignorance or factual disagreement.

Seek out and home in on their false assumptions. Sometimes all it takes to turn someone around is explaining why things aren't what they think they are. After Paul showed the voters how corrupt the incumbent was, the mayor didn't seem like such a great guy any more.

But before you present the facts that support your case, it's a good idea to probe further to determine if that's the main point of disagreement or only a side issue. Asking a question like "If I could show you that this assumption isn't true, would you consider changing your mind?" can save you a lot of time and effort. Otherwise you could find that providing the information you think they need makes no difference at all. When Rose told Jim Doyle he couldn't afford Jefferson Heights, he wanted to see homes there anyway. That told Rose that Doyle had some other Purpose than buying a house and she decided not to spend any more time with him.

Sometimes it's the persuader and not the persuadee who is ignorant and beginning the dialog by questioning and listening may unearth what the actual conflicts are. That's what Alex discovered. He had been prepared to prove he could be trusted with the car only to find that the real issues were his father's sports car and the cost of insurance.

7. Explain why you're right.

When you do present your own case, in addition to following the teaching guidelines in the last chapter, pay special attention to laying out your facts and reasons in a non-threatening way. You want your listener to feel comfortable, safe, and justified in changing his mind but, when people disagree, it's easy to arouse antagonism or put someone on the defensive. You need to communicate objectively and respectfully, and there are several ways to do it.

One is to avoid "you" messages like "You're wrong about [something]" or "You're just trying to give me a hard time." It makes your listener and his deficiencies – even if they really exist – the subject of the discussion. Right away, his Purpose becomes disproving what you just said about him. He may even retaliate by going on offense and finding fault with **you**.

If you don't want that to happen, try using "I" messages like "I came to a different conclusion because ..." or "I agree with you that [something] is important and I think the best way of getting it is ..."

Rose communicated with "I messages" when she told Jim Doyle that she wanted to show him a home he could afford and maybe, someday, one in the expensive neighborhood. So did Alex when he said "I know how much your car means to you, Dad."

Another option is an "It is" statement where you simply and impersonally state the facts. Rose told Doyle what various homes cost and gave him brochures with details about houses in his price range even after she concluded he was being unreasonable.

You could also ask a "Did you know ...?" question. Paul never confronted, attacked, or criticized anyone who thought the mayor was doing a good job. Instead, his "Did you know ...?" questions communicated the facts in a non-threatening way.

So, if you want to help your listeners focus on your facts and reasons without them getting sidetracked and defensive proving they're not stupid, ignorant, or poorly motivated, use "I" messages, "It is" statements, and "Did you know ...?" questions.

During the process of asking and listening, you may conclude that someone can't be persuaded. They may be unwilling or even turn hostile when you ask them what they think and why. They may not have a good reason for their position and maybe they don't care. There's not much you can do about that, except back off and try a more opportune moment, as Alex did, or a better subject for your pitch, as Rose did.

But even someone who will eventually come to agree with you, may not do so right away. That's OK. When it's a matter of deeply held convictions or complex issues, people need time to think it over. If you can effectively communicate your own point of view or get them to question and reconsider theirs, you've succeeded.

CHAPTER 14

Raising a WHYS child

Would you like to raise a WHYS child – a self-confident, purposeful, sensible youngster who understands causes and is well-prepared to succeed in life?

Matt's Mom and Dad did it by giving him **reasons** and explaining **why** right from the beginning.

Infancy

Shoppers at the supermarket didn't know what to make of the one-way conversation Matt's Mom was having with her weeks-old baby in the infant carrier.

"I'm buying these bananas because they're green and Daddy wants bananas to ripen at home. ... I'm getting 10 jars of spaghetti sauce because we use it all the time and they're on sale this week." Almost everything Mom or Dad did in Matt's presence was accompanied by a detailed causal explanation. Matt heard the word "because" more often than the average child hears the word "No."

Toddlerhood

Toilet-training is usually a power struggle between parents eager to get their kid out of diapers and a child in the midst of the "terrible two's." Not in Matt's house because Mom and Dad left it up to their son.

"Here are big boy pants," Mom said, indicating the white cloth training pants in the lowest dresser drawer – the one Matt could open all by himself. "If you want to try using the potty like Daddy does, you can wear them instead of diapers." Then she pointed to the colorful underpants with real fly fronts and pictures of Superman and Teenage Mutant Ninja Turtles on them. "These are Underoos. When you can always pee and poop in the potty, you can wear these."

That's all Matt's parents did. When Matt was good and ready, he toilet-trained himself.

Pre-school

Matt's parents sent him to a Montessori school because they wanted him in an open classroom where he had the freedom to select and direct his own learning in accordance with his own desires and Purposes. The Montessori "prepared environment" was rich with hands-on sensory materials specifically designed to demonstrate the Characteristics of Things and allow for focused Reality Testing. The Montessori "practical life exercises" taught Matt how to perform multi-step tasks like dressing himself and preparing and serving his own food.

Childhood questions

"Why is the sky blue?" "Why do I have to go to the doctor?" Most children ask lots of questions and, when Matt did, his parents were delighted and wanted him to keep it up. They answered his questions as fully as they could and, when they didn't know, they showed him how to find answers in books and from experts.

In addition, they asked **him** questions to get him thinking about causes and reasons. One day five-year-old Matt and his Mom were walking down a steep road.

> "Is it easier to walk down this road or up the road?" Mom asked.
>
> "Down," said Matt.
>
> "Why?" asked Mom.
>
> Matt thought it over for a few minutes and then said "Because things fall down. They don't fall up."

Elementary school

"What can we do about Matthew?" his first grade teacher pleaded. "I told him to do something and, instead of doing it, he just stood there and said 'What for?'"

Mom smiled. "That's the first question he asks about any proposed activity. His father and I always give him a reason when we make a request and he expects one. Nothing will make him act if he doesn't get a 'what for,' but I think if you explain *why* you want him to do something, he'll cooperate."

Once his teacher added a "what for," he did. She also started adding reasons when she asked other children to do things, and they cheerfully complied as well. It turned out to be the best first grade class she had ever taught.

The bike

Mom and Dad vetoed the idea of twelve year-old Matt riding his bike to school. "We aren't ready for you to do that yet because we're worried about your safety. Maybe next year."

Matt disagreed, but instead of arguing, he wrote Mom and Dad a letter. In it he laid out, in detail, his awareness of the potential hazards and how he planned to avoid them. He would stay on the bike path, be aware of traffic, walk his bike across intersections, wear his helmet, lock his bike inside the school gate, etc. Mom and Dad were persuaded and relented.

Reaching for the stars

Matt's parents did everything they could to encourage his developing interests and values. When Matt wanted to play the guitar, they paid for lessons. When he became interested in astronomy at age 15, Dad provided him with a telescope and went to the monthly meetings of the local astronomical society with him. Dad also arranged for Matt to take an astronomy course at a local college where, although he was the youngest student in the class, he earned the highest grade.

Adolescent "rebellion"

The teen years are difficult ones for any family and Matt's was no exception. His Mom and Dad had raised an unusually independent child with his own standards, values, and Purposes which, at times, were at odds with those of his parents.

When Matt wanted to dye his strawberry blond hair black or wear weird clothing, Mom and Dad didn't like it, but they let it go. The hair would grow out. They drew the line at anything that would have permanent consequences like a tattoo, a pregnancy, or an arrest record and they always erred on the side of caution. They gave their reasons, as always, but Matt often objected.

"You can't make me. I don't have to do things your way any more."

"You're right," said his Dad. "You don't have to do things our way. You also don't have to eat our food, sleep in our house, wear clothes we pay for, or any other benefits that come from living here. But as long as you stay in our house, we expect you to follow our rules. When you have your own place and pay your own bills, you can do things differently."

Eventually, Matt did strike out on his own. He got a job in a sales-related field earning top commissions. He gained the trust and respect of many friends of all ages because of his honesty, integrity, passion for values, and sound judgment. When he did get his own place, he set his own rules – and they were very similar to his parents'.

WHYS parenting step by step

If you want to help your child make good choices and take successful actions based on an accurate understanding of causes and effects, here is what you can do.

1. Explain the reasons for your actions.

Whenever you can, explain *why* you're doing what you're doing. Describe, in terms of Things and Characteristics, what facts are guiding your choices and actions. Matt's Mom, in the supermarket, said she was buying the bananas (the Things) because they were green and would ripen at home (their Characteristics) and the spaghetti sauce (the Thing) because it was on sale (a Characteristic).

Give reasons even if your child is too young to understand them. If nothing else, he will learn that you *have* reasons for your actions. It's comforting for a child to know that those he depends on to protect and guide him know what they're doing.

You might over-explain or say too much, but what's the harm? It's better to say too much than too little. Children understand a lot more than you may think and you never know when a child will begin to get it. Even if he doesn't get it all, he will come to realize there's a connection between your purposeful, confident actions and your "becauses." That's the best way to teach the importance and the vital skill of thinking about causes.

2. Explain the reasons for your feelings and emotional reactions.

Instead of praising or condemning your child's actions, use the "I messages" we discussed in the last chapter to explain the reasons why his behavior is important to you. Put it in the form: "I feel (emotion) when I perceive (something he's done) because ..."

Instead of saying things like

"You made the living room a mess."

"You're a talented writer."

try

"I get angry when I see your Legos left all over the living room floor because I'm afraid somebody will step on one and get hurt. They belong in the box when you're not playing with them."

"Your story made me laugh, especially the part about the giant balloon. I enjoy imaginative touches like that."

When you use the "I feel ... because ..." formula, a child doesn't feel overruled, put down, or judged – just informed. It's the best way to teach your child values – especially *moral* standards – because emotions are how we experience our values. The "I feel" part communicates your positive or negative assessment and its degree of importance and the "because ..." part indicates the Things and Characteristics that triggered your emotional reaction.

"I feel ... because ..." not only tells your child how *you* evaluate something and why, but it also shows him how he can perform the crucial process of introspection on his own. It serves as a live demonstration of how to identify and connect *his own* reactions to his values and experiences.

3. Always give reasons for your requests.

When you want your child to do something, give him a "what for." Unlike commands and threats, it may not get you instant, blind obedience, but he won't be scared of you or inwardly seething with resentment either. It's a reasonable, respectful approach that will get you cooperation in the short run and produce a thinking, confident, independent adult in the long run.

4. Answer his questions.

When you know the answer, tell him what it is and why it's true. When you don't know the answer, go on an adventurous information hunt with your child. Look it up in books and on the internet, consult experts, and perform your own experiments.

Even if you can't find the answer you're looking for, you'll be communicating that it's out there for him to discover and you'll show him what he needs to do to find it.

5. Ask him "Why" questions.

Challenge your child with questions about everyday things.

> "Why are you bigger than your brother?"

> "Why does the traffic light change to yellow before it turns red?"

"Asking Why" is a fun game with endless possibilities that teaches your child how to think causally in a "learn by doing" way.

Ask him about the things he likes and dislikes.

> "Which do you like more: Star Trek or Star Wars? Why?"

> "How come you're eating sushi now when you hated it last year?"

This will help your child develop introspection and evaluation skills and, best of all, sharing likes and dislikes enhances your relationship with your child. You'll learn a lot about him and what he wants and he will see that you recognize what's important to him and take it seriously.

6. Show him how to do things.

When you do tasks or engage in activities, show him how you do it. Break the job down into small, manageable steps and invite him to join you as you do them.

7. Nurture his emerging and developing personal values.

Succeeding means achieving one's Purpose. Therefore, the first thing a child needs is to *have* a Purpose, but that's not something you can give him. It has to come from inside the child – from his own wants and needs.

All children need food, clothing, shelter, etc. In addition, early in life a child begins to develop the distinctive, optional personal values that will make him a unique person. He may enjoy music or making things with his hands or sports or movies or karate. The particular value doesn't matter so long as it's *his* value.

Do what you can to give him the opportunity and the means to explore many areas of interest and encourage the ones that appeal to him most. That might mean getting him a catcher's mitt or a second-hand trombone, finding him a teacher or a coach, or taking him camping.

Whatever he wants, urge him to go for it. Some things will be passing interests, but others may become lifelong passions or a productive and satisfying career.

Raising a child The WHYS Way is challenging, but rewarding. While he's growing up, you'll have many joys over the years. Afterward, you'll have a have special bond with your child – now a happy and successful adult.

CHAPTER 15

The WHYS and happy life

Since this is the last chapter, let's review and see how *you* can be happier and more successful by using *The WHYS Way* in *your* life right now.

We began by describing and defining what causes really are: the particular Characteristics of particular Things which make them be what they are and do what they do. Then we explained how you can find causes and how you can use logic to know and prove that you've really got the cause.

After that, we investigated how your mind works when it takes in and later remembers information and how memories of happy and painful experiences produce emotions alerting you to dangers and rewarding you with good feelings.

Then we explored how to apply an understanding of the WHYS to real, practical, everyday issues.

We asked and answered

- How do you achieve your goals – especially the difficult, demanding, and seemingly overwhelming ones?
- What can you do when things go wrong?
- How do you unlock your creative abilities?
- When dealing with other people, how can you make the most of their knowledge, skills, expertise, and advice? Who can you trust and who should you watch out for?
- How can you successfully teach and persuade other people?
- How do you raise a child to be a realistic, sensitive, creative, confident, successful, and happy adult?

We found the answers to these question using the **main idea** of this book:

LIVING A SUCCESSFUL AND HAPPY LIFE
DEPENDS ON UNDERSTANDING THE *WHYS*:
THE CAUSES AND REASONS WHY
THINGS ARE WHAT THEY ARE
AND DO WHAT THEY DO.

The WHYS and happy life step by step

As you've gone from chapter to chapter reading about the WHYS and how to use them, you've encountered these key ideas: Things, Characteristics, Purposes, Reality Testing, the Certainty Test, your Database, Data Mining, Standing Orders, Feel Good Emotions, Feel Bad Emotions, Prep Work, and the Creative Flow.

If you want to make the most of these ideas, here are the steps you can take right now to become a happy and successful WHYS Guy or WHYS Gal.

1. Introspect.

Your emotions contain useful – *although not necessarily reliable* – information about what *may* be good or bad for you and about what things you should go for and what you should avoid. If you think about what you feel and *why*, you can gain important information about the world and about yourself.

As you go through your day, be open and sensitive to what you feel – and not just the big stuff. Pay attention to the little pleasures and little annoyances in your life, too. Then identify the Things and Characteristics that trigger each emotion.

Try this the next time you go to your closet to get something to wear. Notice which clothes you wear all the time and which ones you haven't put on in years. Do you know *why*?

Look at one item, let's say your favorite pair of jeans. How do you *feel* about them? You like them. *Why* do you like them? Look at the jeans and try to name the Characteristics that make you feel that way. They're so comfortable. *Why*? What Characteristics of the jeans makes them so comfy? Maybe it's because the fit is just a tiny bit loose and the denim has softened with wear. Next there's that jacket you never wear any more. *Why* don't you like it? It's "too old." *Why*? Your favorite jeans are three years old and you bought that jacket only six months ago. Focus on the Characteristics of the jacket that make it seem old. You see that the surface of the material is rough and pilling and the zipper is rather scrunched up and doesn't lay flat. You loved the jacket when you first bought it but, after a few washings, it didn't look so good anymore.

Going through your closet while identifying your feelings and the Characteristics of the Things that cause them has benefits. The Things and Characteristics you just identified will be stored in your Database for future reference. The next time you're buying jeans you'll be more aware of the fit and the softness of the material. When you find a shirt you like, you may ask yourself, "Yeah, but what will it look like after I wash it ten times?"

As you go through your day, pay attention to your Feel Good Emotions, especially the little pleasures. *Why* do you like your first cup of coffee in the morning so much? You always like the taste of coffee, but that first cup is special. *Why?* You associate it with the promise of a new day. *Why?* Because that's when you sit down at your desk, sip your coffee, and plan out what you're going to do today. Then you realize how important taking time to plan is.

Now let's consider Feel Bad Emotions. It's hard to ignore major Feel Bad Emotions like fear and anger. They come after you, grab your attention, and impel you to do something right now. But also pay attention to your more subtle Feel Bad Emotions – the *little* pains and fears and guilts. These less intense feelings are important because, although they're easier to ignore, they can chip away, little by little, at your self-esteem and your enjoyment of life.

Be sensitive to, and identify, the messages underlying them. The sadness you feel when hearing a friend's name could mean "I miss him." The fear might be "Maybe he doesn't like me anymore." The guilt could be "I should have called him." Once you get the messages and Reality Test them, you might decide that there's no reason to conclude your friend doesn't like you and it would be a good idea for you to call him right now.

Introspecting makes you more **aware** of what you want and don't want and **why**. That's crucial information that will guide you toward making **better choices**. So, if you want to fill your life with Things that will make you happy, pay attention to how you feel about the Things in your life *now* and **identify the reasons why** you feel as you do.

2. Identify.

When you introspect *The WHYS Way*, you're identifying – **in words** – what you feel, the messages contained in your feelings, and the Things and Characteristics that triggered your emotional reactions. Then you Reality

Test the messages and, if they are true and relevant, you have a Purpose and you're *almost* ready to take action.

Should you state your Purpose in words? You may not have to if it's a simple matter. If your finger itches, you just scratch it without further thought. But if something big is at stake or you have the slightest Feel Bad Emotion or emotional conflict, it's a good idea to consciously state your Purposes and goals in words.

Let's say you're hungry and you want to eat something. You see the candy dish and you start moving in that direction. Then you feel a twinge of guilt. *Why?* Putting your feelings into words you get "I shouldn't eat it. It's just empty calories." You move away from the candy but then you feel deprived. *Why?* Putting that into words you get "I'm hungry. I want something sweet," and then you add "that isn't all sugar." That's just the search key your Data Miner needs. The desire whose message is "Get an apple" pops out of your Database. You Reality Test it, find no contradictions or emotional conflicts, and you go and get an apple.

3. Let your Purpose be your guide.

Once you know what you want and have put your desires into words and Reality Tested them, you'll have a Purpose – and we've seen how important that is. Without a Purpose, you'd be lost and anxious, wanting something you weren't quite sure of and not knowing what to do next. Having a Purpose gives you a direction so you can confidently take action. A Purpose plus a deadline for achieving it gives you a *goal*.

Your Purpose helps you select the particular Things you'll need. If you're planning a camping trip in the wilderness, you might bring a tent, a sleeping bag, a backpack, etc. – but not a microwave oven. Your Purpose will also help you select the Characteristics those Things should have. If you'll be hiking ten miles to the campsite, you'd probably be concerned with the size and weight of the gear you'll be carrying but not with its color.

Your purpose keeps you moving toward what you want. They say a journey of a thousand miles begins with a single step. That's a lot of steps! How can you be sure you won't get lost along the way? You won't if you use your Purpose as a compass to point you toward your ultimate goal. As you follow it, you'll know that you're headed in the right direction and that each step will take you closer to your destination. Even if you encounter an obstacle in your path and have to detour around it, your Purpose will point the way to getting back on track.

Your Purpose helps you break down a large, difficult, and complex goal into manageable, doable steps. Imagine that your house is a mess and company's coming. You feel exhausted just thinking about cleaning it all up. What can you do? You can do a small *part* of the job. Clean the dining room. Still too much? How about just removing the junk that doesn't belong on the dining table? That's a step in the right direction and it will only take a few minutes. Once that's done, you feel pretty good. You've accomplished *something* that gets you closer to your goal. The pleasure motivates you to keep going and the small act of straightening up the dining table gives you momentum to continue.

When you have a clear Purpose, you'll know when you can stop. You don't have to worry about making it "perfect" if you know, before you begin, what you want to do and what you need to know. As soon as you've achieved your Purpose, that's good enough and you're done.

4. Plan.

Once you have your Purpose clearly in mind, you can lay out a path to your goal. Break the job down into steps. Make a list of tasks and a list of Things you'll need. If you can't hold this in your head, write it down. You'll make efficient use of your time and not forget anything if you head out the door with a written list like this:

Library – return books

Goodwill store – leave donation

Supermarket – milk, eggs, coffee, ground beef, onions

Observe that your simple plan takes causes, effects, Things, and their Characteristics into account. You need to return the books now or you'll have to pay a fine. The food shopping is left for last because you're buying some perishable items and you want to get them home and into your refrigerator as soon as possible.

Should you always have a plan? Yes, even if it's only implicit. It keeps you on track and prevents you from wasting time and effort. What about leisure activities and taking time off? Should you plan that too? Yes!

You can't fully relax and let yourself go when there's the nagging, guilty thought: "I ought to be doing (something else)." It's better to make sure beforehand that there isn't anything more important you can and should be doing. Schedule a block of time when you can indulge in your favorite activity or just goof off with a clear conscience. Then enjoy!

5. Evaluate and measure.

Evaluate the Characteristics of the Things you're dealing with. Is your job (Thing) getting boring (Characteristic)? What item on the menu (Thing) looks the most appealing (Characteristic)? Where can you get the best price (Characteristic) on your new car (Thing)?

As you go about your day, pause briefly from time to time to measure and evaluate how you're doing. Are you running late? Did you get feedback from your sales prospect indicating he understood your product's benefits? Will you have time to finish planting before it gets dark? Reality Test your work-in-process and you'll know when you're on track and when you need to change your plans.

Evaluating and measuring makes you more **aware** of Things and Characteristics that matter most to you. Instead of bumbling through life pushed and pulled by unknown forces and unexamined feelings, take charge of your life by **knowing** what you're doing and how it's going.

6. Interact - Trade, share, learn, teach, and persuade.

Make the most of your social interactions. Seek out the people who have the Characteristics that add value to your life. Look for honest people of good character you can trust, admire, respect, befriend, and love. Find knowledgeable, intelligent teachers and experts you can learn from. Hire people with the skills you need. Sell your products and services to customers who want them and buy from sellers offering what you want.

Respect the fact that other people have Purposes that can be quite different from yours and take this into account when you deal with them. Bring up subjects that you have a reason to believe will serve *their* Purposes as well as yours. If you and your neighbor are both avid gardeners, she might like to hear about the sale at the garden center. She'd probably be less inclined to listen to a half-hour rant about what's wrong with candidate Elvin Meister if her lawn sports a "Meister for Senate" sign.

Enhance your relationships by *identifying* the Characteristics that you like in friends and lovers and then *telling* them. The man who is constantly telling his wife "I love the way your hair frames your face," and "Thanks for being so nice to my cousin," and "Your casserole was delicious" will have a wife who feels seen, appreciated, and loved.

7. Optimize.

Look for little improvements you can make. How can you change the Characteristics of the Things you use every day to increase your comfort and enjoyment or to save you time, effort and money? How about trying new herbs and spices when you cook and see if the food tastes better? If you hate lacing up your shoes, why not wear loafers? Can you increase your gas mileage or get a closer shave? Could you save time by rearranging what's in your kitchen cabinets?

If your life is good, make it even better.

8. Seek greater certainty and clarity.

All through your life you've reached conclusions about thousands and thousands of things. If you've done it *The WHYS Way*, you have very good reasons for your opinions.

But not all of your conclusions are the same. Some you're absolutely sure of and they pass the Certainty Test. As for the rest of your assumptions, you have *some* evidence that they are true and that may be sufficient for your Purposes. Note, however, that you can act with greater confidence when you're completely *sure* of what you're doing.

For instance, you know that you got a good deal on your computer because it had all the necessary Characteristics. It was a top-rated model with all the features you wanted. You bought it brand new with a full warranty for 20% less than the next lowest price quoted anywhere. That's why you don't worry that maybe you should have shopped around more before buying it.

But are you as confident of everything you do?

What about your *basic* ideas about what's right and good? You probably learned them from your parents and teachers when you were a child and you never had cause to question or doubt them. But since your most important actions are affected by the moral ideals you accept and practice, it's a good idea to seek a deeper understanding of *why* they are true whenever you have the chance.

Why do you believe what you do and what Things and Characteristics is it based on? Think about your beliefs concerning what is right and good until you're certain. Knowing *why* you're doing the right thing will give you moral clarity and confidence.

What is a happy life? It's a life filled with happy experiences, goals achieved, and desires satisfied. They could be some major but rare joyful events, but usually it comes from making *steps* toward your goals. It comes from small daily pleasures happening one after another, that give you the sense that all's right with the world and that you're a rather terrific person.

Big problems or little annoyances don't faze you because you regard them as normal happenings on the way to getting what you want. You deal with them confidently realizing that you have what it takes to handle anything life throws at you.

If your ultimate Purpose in life is to be happy, pay attention to what you want, identify and Reality Test your desires and Purposes, identify the Characteristics of the Things you'll use as you make step by step plans to achieve your goals, deal with and overcome problems as they arise, and measure your progress as you keep moving closer and closer to what you want.

That's the way to success and happiness – and now you know WHY.

Acknowledgements

I'm grateful to the many people who helped me with this book.

First, I'd like to thank my father, Henry Biderman. He was a successful entrepreneur who faced life with the bouncing enthusiasm of a child. I idolized him and, as I made my way into the wider world, I discovered how rare people like my dad were. I decided that finding out why he was so happy and successful was something crucially important because I wanted to grow up to be happy and successful too.

While both my parents encouraged me to make the most of my abilities and accomplish great things, my dad was the biggest influence. I watched what my father did. I constantly asked him why he did what he did and he always had an answer that made sense. I came to him when I wanted something and he showed me how to get it. Little by little I adopted his approach to life and it worked.

From the age of seven on I earned money all by myself and got the things I wanted – a bicycle, a camera, a tape recorder, and a college education. I did small jobs for others and started little businesses. I got straight A's, not because I studied hard and memorized, but because I was immensely curious and was able to figure things out.

Always on the lookout for people who saw life the way my dad and I did, I sought out and found a few more. Especially important was Ayn Rand. When I first read her novels at age 18, I immediately recognized that her heroes were "my kinda people." I investigated further to learn as much as I could about what she advocated and if and why it was true.

In an authorized biography of Ayn Rand, I read:

> [At about age 12,] a change was occurring in Ayn's approach to ideas and method of thinking – a change which fascinated and absorbed her. She called her new method: thinking in principles. She had held definite convictions before, but now – in a major step toward adulthood – she began to formulate her ideas in conscious, conceptual terms; **she began to construct abstract logical chains of "Why's,"** to identify the deepest **reasons** of her convictions, to ask herself, about all the issues of her concern, what she believed, and **why**. [Emphasis mine.][16]

That's what my dad and I were doing!

But my dad wasn't, ultimately, the most important man in my life. When I was 22, I met and married Stephen Speicher. If there ever was a "WHYS Guy," it was Stephen. I've never seen anything like his tenacity in seeking out what was true. He was a pioneer in computer telecommunications, a mathematical innovator whose equations are used to calculate the effects of nuclear explosions, and an internationally respected authority on Einstein's theories. At Caltech he invented methods and computer tools used in the Human Genome Project and stem cell research. Best of all, he had the same passionate, playful spirit as my dad. It was a delight to share my life with him.

Stephen always encouraged me to do and be my best and the fact that I wrote this book is a tribute to him. It's too bad he couldn't live to read it, but his spirit is in every page.

When I began to write this book, the job seemed overwhelming. I'd write a couple of chapters and get stuck. Then I took Gene Perret's course on how to write and finish a book and that got me unstuck. Gene has since turned his course into a book titled *Write Your Book Now!: A Proven System to Start and FINISH the Book You've Always Wanted to Write!*[17] I heartily recommend it.

As I wrote *The WHYS Way*, I had the ongoing help and encouragement of my friends and fellow writers at the Goebel Center in Thousand Oaks. What a talented bunch! We meet on Thursdays to read and critique each other's work and their feedback was invaluable. I'd especially like to thank our "fearless leader" Laurie Greene. Her eagle eyes caught every dangling participle and other grammatical lapses but, best of all, she could spot passages that were unclear or didn't quite fit with the rest of what I was trying to say.

Others also read and gave me suggestions that improved the finished book. Thanks to Alan Nitikman, Shoshana Milgram, Lisa Doby, Jordan Philips, Domingo Garcia, Eric Kalin, and Corey Woods.

I'd also like to thank my "tracking partner," Gregory Zeigerson. Greg is a cartoonist and all-around creative guy who wanted to do various artistic projects. I wanted to finish my book. We contacted each other daily to report on what we had accomplished in the previous day and our plans for the next day. This arrangement helped us both with our respective projects. Greg is also a professional proofreader who caught many of my typos.

When the book was all written and edited, I turned it over to a master graphic designer: my sister Marsha Biderman. Marsha is a pro who has put together books for Springhouse Publications and J. P. Lippincott. I am so fortunate to have her give my work the look and style I want it to have.

In addition to my father and my husband Stephen, this book is dedicated to my son, Matthew. Matt is the future, my Purpose, and the "what for?" behind the writing of this book. Just as I learned *The WHYS Way* from my dad, Matt learned it from his father and me. The result has been wonderful. Matt is a capable and successful young man who knows what he wants and how to get it.

That's what I want for everyone and that's why I wrote this book.

End Notes

[1] Ambrose, Susan A., Bridges, Michael W., et. al. (2010). *How Learning Works: Seven Research-Based Principles for Smart Teaching.* Jossey-Bass. p. 19, ISBN 0470484101.

[2] Damer, T Edward (1995). *Attacking Faulty Reasoning: A Practical Guide to Fallacy-Free Arguments* (3rd. ed.). Belmont, CA: Wadsworth Publishing. p. 131. ISBN 978-0-534-21750-1. OCLC 30319422.

[3] Hume, David. *An Enquiry Concerning Human Understanding*, sect. VII., p. 62.

[4] Hume, David, *A Treatise of Human Nature*, Book 1, Part 3, Section 14 - "Of the Idea of Necessary Connection"

[5] Kanbar, Maurice (2001). *Secrets from an Inventor's Notebook.* Council Oak Books. p. 26-27. ISBN 1-57178-099-8.

[6] Aristotle, *Metaphysics*, (1005b 19-20)

[7] Aristotle, *Metaphysics* 7, (1011b 26-27)

[8] Aristotle, *Metaphysics*, (Book IV, Part 7)

[9] Lorayne, Harry and Lucas, Jerry (1974). *The Memory Book.* Barnes and Noble Books. p. 89. ISBN 0-88029-322-5.

[10] In-Depth: Cognitive Behavioral Therapy, Ben Martin, Psy.D., http://psychcentral.com/lib/in-depth-cognitive-behavioral-therapy/000907

[11] Perret, Gene (2011). *Write Your Book Now!: A Proven System to Start and FINISH the Book You've Always Wanted to Write!*, Quill Driver Books. p. 14. ISBN 1610350065.

[12] Peikoff, Leonard edited by Trollope, Marlene (2014). *Teaching Johnny to Think: A Philosophy of Education Based on the Principles of Ayn Rand's Objectivism*, Ayn Rand Institute Press,. ISBN 9780979466168.

[13] Ibid., p. 20.

[14] Ibid., p. 21.

[15] Ibid.

[16] Branden, Nathaniel and Barbara (1962). *Who is Ayn Rand?.* Random House. p. 159, ISBN 0394451791.

[17] Perret, Gene (2011). Op. Cit.

Made in the USA
Charleston, SC
03 October 2016